Favourite Prayers

Favourite Prayers

CHOSEN BY PEOPLE FROM ALL WALKS OF LIFE

Compiled by
Deborah Cassidi

CASSELL

Cassell
Wellington House
125 Strand, London WC2R 0BB
370 Lexington Avenue, New York, NY 10017-6550

First published 1998

British Library Cataloguing-in-Publication Data
A catalogue record for this book is available from the British Library.

ISBN 0-304-70315-x

Illustrations by Jackie Cundall

Designed by Geoff Green
Typeset by Geoff Green Book Design
Printed and bound in Great Britain by
Biddles Ltd, Guildford and King's Lynn

Contents

To my mother, Dr Kathleen Bliss, who helped to found the World Council of Churches and believed passionately in the equality of man, and to my sister, Gillian Barnett, who worked for her community in London.

My thanks to the many contributors, to my long-suffering friends and family and to Judy, Linda, Jackie, Sarah, Audrey, Freda, Paddy, and, in particular, to my husband. This book would not have been possible without their help.

The Lord's Prayer

Our Father, who art in heaven, hallowed be thy name;
thy kingdom come; thy will be done,
on earth as it is in heaven.
Give us this day our daily bread.
And forgive us our trespasses,
as we forgive those who trespass against us.
And lead us not into temptation; but deliver us from evil.
For thine is the kingdom, the power, and the glory,
for ever and ever.

Amen.

I commend this book of favourite prayers which Deborah Cassidi has compiled from the choices of a very wide selection of contributors and I hope that many will find it inspirational and comforting. There is something for everyone within its pages.

Sir John Wills, Lord Lieutenant of Somerset

Foreword

A breath of fresh air blows through this book of prayers. They are blissfully unsystematic. One of the best echoes the theme of a French classic, 'Abandonment to Divine Providence' by Jean Pierre de Caussade.[1] You could say there was an air of abandon about what has been put before us; but it would be a mistake to think of it as a kind of lucky dip. There is something for everyone but the result is an almost miraculously creative mixture.

Deborah Cassidi is, amongst much else, an ophthalmologist. She has certainly looked around with discernment and drawn in a rich haul from many friends and well-chosen names. It is full of memorable nuggets from obscure sources. I like the traditional prayer of the Manx fishermen or the brisk poetic immediacy of Beth Chatto's 'Prayer for Rain'. Then there are the old familiar prayers which can still catch us like a net and put us down before the living God. There is wit – but they are mercifully free from confected jokiness – humour on the outskirts of faith gives us a sense of proportion. People without it should never be put in charge of anything. So it needs to be nourished in prayers that smile; but there is no laughter in the inner places of tragedy where the absurdities and incongruities of life are confronted. Roy Calne speaks from the angle of the sensitive surgeon who has been up against the tragedies often enough; and Martin Israel (see Fiona Fraser's selection) from the profundity of his spiritual direction.

---

[1] This book has been published under a variety of titles, for example, *Abandonment or Absolute Surrender to Divine Providence* (Washbourne, London, 1887) and *Self-abandonment to Divine Providence* (London, Burns and Oates, 1959).

Deborah Cassidi's mother, to whom the book is dedicated, was one of the most underestimated theologians of this century. I once heard her say, at a service for Christian Unity, 'We are now confronted with the problems of answered prayer. God has opened so many doors but who has the courage to go through them?' There can be few who will read this book without pausing and feeling a door has been opened. I hope that many will find it a good companion and will be encouraged to give even more to develop the Threshold Prize to encourage imaginative writing by children. This collection of people reaching out to God and the aspirations of the young writer make a good partnership. 'Yearning', said Augustine, 'makes the heart deep.'

The Rt. Revd Lord Runcie

The Making of the Anthology

Compiling this anthology has been a celebration of prayer. The main pillars of the book are the contributors themselves; many of them are public figures, those who have excelled in their field or endured much. Other contributions come from Somerset and represent the measured pace of rural life, yet others from around the UK and especially from Lambeth, lying close to the City of London and Westminster. The children's prayers come from East Anglia, Somerset and Northern Ireland. Each contributor was asked to choose a favourite prayer, or in some cases to write one.

The prayers are arranged chiefly in alphabetical order of contributor. When a prayer came from more than one contributor, I allocated it to the first nominator, adding other names as they came in. It was decided at the outset only to use titles and honours coming before the name; this had the advantage of simplicity but it saddened me that some awards for bravery and honours of distinction were left out. I apologize for this and hope I will be forgiven. One happy result of the alphabetical arrangement is that the names jostle together like some giant celebratory street party.

Comments by the contributors appear in quotation marks; my own editorial remarks are preceded by the symbol ¶. The author or source, when known, follows each prayer, and publication details are given in the Acknowledgements on p.156. Sadly, due to the variability of sources and the constraints of space and copyright, it was not always possible to include the full text or particular wording supplied by the contributor.

To write a prayer oneself or choose a favourite, whether for its spiritual meaning, the beauty of its language, its humour, its evocation of memories or as an outline of a precept for life, is to open a small window on oneself; so the reader may well share with me the feelings of privilege and of gratitude to the contributors.

Four main themes run through the book: peace and reconciliation, the triumph of faith and the human spirit over adversity and death, our appreciation of and responsibility for the natural world and finally humour, the sort of leavening humour that laughs at ourselves.

I received messages of support from many people, including Archbishop Tutu and the astronaut, Commander Borman. A dear friend sent a packet of small confetti angels with her prayer, which worked their way between the prayers and into the bills. I was even sent a photograph of a famous footballer holding a bag of crisps. I recently asked Lord Owen for a copyright source for his prayer. 'Copyright?' he retorted. 'I thought prayers belonged to God!' Indeed they do, but Caesar sometimes asks for a levy, so I was truly grateful to the many people who waived their fee.

I make no apology that the prayers are predominantly Christian nor that other faiths are included. I have broken the alphabetical rule by using the Abbot of Downside's choice as an introductory prayer. This is followed by Prince Philip's prayer, written by himself; it gives a lead from the laity and admirably illustrates one of the four main themes of the book.

Deborah Cassidi

Introductory Prayer

The Rt. Revd Charles Fitzgerald-Lombard OSB, *the Abbot of Downside Abbey*

Be not afraid to pray – to pray is right.
Pray, if thou canst, with hope; but ever pray,
Though hope be weak, or sick with long delay;
Pray in the darkness if there be no light.
Far is the time, remote from human sight,
When war and discord on the earth shall cease;
Yet every prayer for universal peace
Avails the blessed time to expedite.
Whate'er is good to wish, ask that of Heaven,
Though it be what thou canst not hope to see;
Pray to be perfect, though material leaven
Forbid the spirit so on earth to be:
> But if for any wish thou darest not pray,
> Then pray to God to cast that wish away.

Hartley Coleridge (1796–1849)

O   Lord, the creator of the universe and author of the laws of nature, inspire in us thy servants the will to ensure the survival of all the species of animals and plants, which you have given to share this planet with us. Help us to understand that we have a responsibility for them and that 'having dominion' does not mean that you have given us the right to exploit the living world without thought for the consequences. Through him who taught us that Solomon in all his glory could not compare with the beauty of the flowers of the field.

Philip

The Duchess of Abercorn

➤►◄◄

Serenity

God grant me the serenity to accept
the things I cannot change,
courage to change the things I can,
and wisdom to know the difference.

Attributed to, but never claimed by, Reinhold Niebuhr (1892–1971).
Probably eighteenth century or earlier

❡ This prayer, Drake's prayer and St Francis of Assisi's prayer 'Make me an instrument of your peace…' were the most often suggested for this anthology.

Also chosen by:
Fred Edwards, *retired Director of Social Work, now engaged in ecology, conservation, kirk and ecumenical matters, who says, 'I am very fond of this prayer and use it a great deal. It is also used by Alcoholics Anonymous throughout the world to conclude meetings';*
Andrew Gailey, *school housemaster, for whom it was chosen 'by a student of mine, Ben Roughton, who despite facing terminal illness, expressed undiminished fascination for the wonder of life';*
Tony and Linda Jackson, *Somerset birdwatchers;*
David Shattock, *Chief Constable of Avon and Somerset Police.*

Sir Antony Acland, *Provost of Eton College*

→>◄←

Grant us, O Lord, the Royalty of inward happiness and the serenity that comes from living close to Thee. Daily renew in us the sense of joy, and let Thy eternal spirit dwell in our souls and bodies, filling every corner of our hearts with light and gladness. So that, bearing about with us the infection of a good courage, we may be diffusers of life, and meet all that comes, of good or ill, even death itself, with gallant and high-hearted happiness; giving Thee thanks always for all things.

Robert Louis Stevenson (1850–94)

'A prayer for those brave people who remain cheerful under adversity when courage is indeed infectious.'

❡ Used at the services of the Order of St Michael and St George.

Kriss Akabusi, *Olympic athlete*

→>◄←

A Bag of Tools

Isn't it strange that princes and kings
And clowns that caper in sawdust rings
And ordinary folk like you and me
Are builders of eternity?

To each is given a book of rules,
An hour glass and a bag of tools.
Each must build ere their time has flown
A stumbling block … or a stepping stone.

R. L. Sharpe

❡ A slightly different version of this poem appears in *Best-loved Poems of the American People*, edited by Hazel Felleman (Doubleday, 1936), but the author R. L. Sharpe could not be traced.

H. R. H. Princess Alexandra

Heaven's not a rest;
No! but to battle with new zest,
Untired, with warrior joy,
The sharp keen spirit to employ
On life's new enterprise.
It's the surprise
Of keen delighted mind
That wakes, to find
Old fetters gone,
Strong shining immortality put on.

Anon.

¶ Princess Alexandra noted this prayer from those used for the memorial service for
Sir Christopher Soames. It was given to the Soames family by a priest, an old family
friend, but its original source is not known.

H. R. H. Princess Alia Al Hussein of Jordan

In the Name of God, the Compassionate, the Merciful.
Praise be to God, Lord of the Worlds,
The Compassionate, the Merciful,
Master of the day of Judgement.
You we worship and of you we ask help.
Guide us upon the straight path;
The path of those whom you have blessed;
Not of those who have incurred your wrath
Nor of those who have gone astray.

'The opening prayer of the Quran is our most read Muslim prayer, as it is a
ritual prayer and also used to bless marriages, and on behalf of those who
pass away, and just for its own sake too.'

Peter Aliss, *professional golfer and TV commentator*

→>-<←

Fear knocked at the door. Faith opened it and there was no one
there.

'This is the family saying at times of adversity but the source is unknown.'

Lady Allen, *housewife*

→>-<←

Each day and night I feel Your presence.
You may not be near to touch,
But You are in my mind and heart.
You meet my needs so silently,
I am never alone, because of You.

'This was given to me by a friend, and was thought to be by Kahlil Gibran.'

Elizabeth Allsop, *farm smallholder (mixed stock)*

→>-<←

Newness of Life

O most merciful Father, for Thy most innocent Son's sake: and
since He has spread His arms upon the cross, to receive the whole
world, O Lord, shut out none of us (who are now fallen before the
throne of Thy majesty and Thy mercy) from the benefit of His
merits; but with as many of us as begin their conversion and
newness of life this minute, this minute, O God, begin Thou Thy
account with them and put all that is past out of Thy remembrance.
Accept our humble thanks for all Thy mercies; and continue and
enlarge them upon the whole church.

John Donne (1572–1631)

'Donne was so aware of the need and availability of redemption for the
repentant and so endearingly immediate: "this minute, this minute".'

Jeffrey and Mary Archer, *politician/author and scientist*

→>-<+

Blessed art Thou, O Lord our God, who makes the bands of sleep to fall upon mine eyes, and slumber upon mine eyelids. May it be Thy will, O Lord my God, to suffer me to lie down in peace and to let me rise up again in peace. Let not my thoughts trouble me, nor evil dreams, nor evil fancies, but let my rest be perfect before Thee. Amen.

Hebrew Prayer-book

¶ Lord and Lady Archer also sent 'the Master Carpenter Prayer' (see Archbishop Carey) as well as this general prayer, often used at a funeral.

Lord Armstrong, *retired civil servant*

→>-<+

Almighty God, the fountain of all wisdom, who knowest our necessities before we ask, and our ignorance in asking; We beseech thee to have compassion upon our infirmities; and those things, which for our unworthiness we dare not, and for our blindness we cannot ask, vouchsafe to give us, for the worthiness of thy Son Jesus Christ our Lord. Amen.

Communion Service, Book of Common Prayer

'Why do I like it? For its balance between God's worthiness, his knowledge and his wisdom, and man's unworthiness, his ignorance and his blindness, and for its simplicity and directness. It has been set to music by Thomas Tomkins in a motet of great beauty.'

The Rt. Hon. Paddy Ashdown, *MP*

➤➤◄◄

We thank Thee, O Lord, that Thou art in every place, that no space or distance can ever separate us from Thee. That those who are absent from each other are still present in Thee. Have in Thy holy keeping all those from whom we are separated and grant that we, by drawing closer to Thee, may be drawn closer to each other.

'A family prayer said nightly when we are parted. Another prayer which I sometimes use, but more as a jest than anything else, I describe as "An old politician's prayer".'

Lord, make my words sweet and reasonable. For some day I may have to eat them!

Vice-Admiral Sir Peter Ashmore

➤➤◄◄

He that dwelleth in the secret place of the most High shall abide
    under the shadow of the Almighty.
I will say of the Lord, He is my refuge and my fortress: my God; in
    him will I trust.
He shall call upon me, and I will answer him: I will be with him in
    trouble; I will deliver him and honour him.

Psalm 91, verses 1, 2 and 15 (Authorized Version)

'The entire psalm is the Christian's sheet anchor in times of deepest trouble. To say or read it slowly brings confidence, peace and a consciousness of God's presence.'

¶ See also the translation chosen by John Conteh.

Carol Auger, *Lambeth street market stall-holder*

━➤━◄━

Dear Lord and Father of mankind,
Forgive our foolish ways!
Re-clothe us in our rightful mind,
In purer lives thy service find.
In deeper reverence praise.

J. G. Whittier (1807–92)

'I like to say this last thing at night.'

Professor M. A. Zaki Badawi, *Principal of the Muslim College UK*

━➤━◄━

The Prayer of the Oppressed

O God, I place before You my weakness, my helplessness and the little esteem that people have of me. O Most Merciful God, You are Lord of the Oppressed and You are my Lord. Into whose hands will You entrust me? To a stranger who will ill-treat me? Or to an enemy whom you have empowered against me? Even if You so will, it will not matter to me so long as You are not angry with me … There is no power or strength except through You.

Translated by M. A. Zaki Badawi from the collection of the Prophetic Hadith.

'This was the Prophet's supplication to God at the moment when he was rejected and stoned by his enemies and forced to take refuge in an orchard.'

The Very Revd Peter Baelz,
Dean Emeritus of Durham Cathedral

→>–<←

Beneath this slab
John Brown is stowed.
He watched the ads
and not the road.

Ogden Nash (1902–71)

Lord, where we are wrong
make us willing to change
And where we are right
make us easy to live with.

Peter Marshall (1903–39)

'This prayer hangs in our kitchen cupboard. My wife put it there. I wonder
what (whom) she had in mind.'

❡ The Very Revd Peter Baelz, author of the prayer sent by Katherine Venning,
responded to a request for an epitaph or grace with these two pieces.

Rear-Admiral John Barker, *Chairman of the*
International World Youth Sailing Committee

→>–<←

Guide us, teach us and strengthen us, O Lord, we beseech Thee,
until we become such as Thou wouldst have us be: pure, gentle,
truthful, courteous, generous, dutiful, useful and above all valiant,
in all our doings; for Thy honour and glory. Amen.

The Revd Charles Kingsley (1819–75)

Priscilla Barker, *housewife*

✦

Give us, O God, the vision which can see Thy love in the world in spite of human failure. Give us the faith to trust Thy goodness in spite of our ignorance and weakness. Give us the knowledge that we continue to pray with understanding hearts, and to do what each one of us can do to set forward the coming of the day of universal peace. Amen.

A prayer offered in space on Christmas Eve, 1968,
by *Apollo VIII*'s commander, Frank Borman

¶ Commander Borman, who wrote this prayer, later became a lay reader for the Episcopalian Church. He sent his good wishes with the permission for its inclusion in this anthology.

Michael Barnett, *artist*

✦

Please think through me,
feel through me,
speak through me,
act through me,
love through me.
I surrender, trust and accept
whatever comes today like it or not.

Phyllis Krystal

¶ Phyllis Krystal writes that she received this prayer during meditation. It is published in *Cutting More Ties That Bind* (Element Books).

Lady Bates, *architect*

+>-<+-

The Fisherman's Prayer

God grant that I may live to fish
Until my dying day
And when it comes to my last cast
I then most humbly pray
When in the Lord's safe landing net
I'm peacefully asleep
That in his mercy I be judged
As good enough to keep.

Anon.

Also chosen by:
Annette Gage, *pancake-maker.*

Sir Dawson Bates Bt, *retired land agent*

+>-<+-

O Lord, our heavenly Father, Almighty and everlasting God, who hast safely brought us to the beginning of this day; Defend us in the same with thy mighty power; and grant that this day we fall into no sin, neither run into any kind of danger; but that all our doings may be ordered by thy governance, to do always that is righteous in thy sight; through Jesus Christ our Lord. Amen.

Morning Prayer, the third Collect, for Grace, Book of Common Prayer

Mary Berry, *cookery writer*

→>-<-

Bless my kitchen, Lord,
I love its every nook
And bless me as I do my work
Wash pots and pans and cook.

May the meals that I prepare
Be seasoned from above
With thy blessing and thy grace
But most of all thy love.

As we partake of earthly food,
The table thou hast spread,
We'll not forget to thank thee, Lord,
For all our daily bread.

So bless my kitchen, Lord,
And those who enter in.
May they find naught but joy and peace
And happiness therein.

A kitchen prayer, source unknown

Also chosen by:
Winifred Myers, *retired head cook, House of Lords.*

The Rt. Hon. Tony Blair, *Prime Minister*

-+>-<+-

A Psalm of the Sons of Korah

God is our refuge and strength,
A very present help in trouble.

Therefore we will not fear,
 Even though the earth be removed,
 And though the mountains be carried into the midst of the sea;

Though its waters roar and be troubled,
 Though the mountains shake with its swelling.

He makes wars cease to the end of the earth;
He breaks the bow and cuts the spear in two;
He burns the chariot in the fire.

Be still, and know that I am God.

Psalm 46, verses 1, 2, 3, 9 and 10 (New King James Version of the Bible)

Colonel John Blashford-Snell, *explorer and scientist*

→>⋅<←

O Lord God, when Thou givest to Thy servants to endeavour any great matter, grant us to know that it is not the beginning, but the continuing of the same unto the end, until it be thoroughly finished, which yieldeth the true glory: through Him who for the finishing of Thy work laid down His life, our Redeemer Jesus Christ. Amen.

Sir Francis Drake (*c.* 1540–96)

'I chose this because it was very much on my mind when launching Operation Drake in 1978 and Operation Raleigh. It is said that there are no atheists before battle. Imagining how Drake felt, I hoped it would help us also to succeed. Indeed it did!'

Also chosen by:
Mary Bates, Sir Desmond Cassidi, Sir Michael Layard *and* **Sir Jeremy Morse.**

Hugh Blenkin,
Commander Metropolitan Police, retired

→>‹‹-

Footprints

One night a man had a dream. He dreamed he was walking along the beach with the Lord. Across the sky flashed scenes from his life. For each scene, he noticed two sets of footprints in the sand; one belonging to him, and the other to the Lord.

When the last scene of his life flashed before him he looked back at the footprints in the sand. He noticed that many times along the path of his life there was only one set of footprints. He also noticed that it happened at the very lowest and saddest times in his life.

This really bothered him and he questioned the Lord about it. 'Lord, you said that once I decided to follow you, you would walk with me all the way. But I have noticed that during the most troublesome times in my life, there is only one set of footprints. I don't understand why, when I needed you most, you would leave me?'

The Lord replied, 'My precious, precious child, I love you and I would never leave you. During your times of trial and suffering, when you see only one set of footprints, it was then that I carried you.'

Anon.

'I was sent this when in hospital with a grave illness; it was a great help, and I really was "carried" through a difficult time.'

Also chosen by:
Major William Pearson-Gee, *Coldstream Guards, father of Jamie, who died when very young.*

Phyllis Bliss, *bassoonist, mathematician and teacher*

Lead me, Lord, lead me in Thy righteousness.
Make thy way plain before my face.
For it is thou, Lord, only who makest me dwell in safety.

Psalms 5, verse 8, and 4, verse 8 (Authorized Version)

'This was beautifully set to music by Samuel Sebastian Wesley (1810–76), a leading Victorian organist, eccentric, and grandson of Charles Wesley. It was the favourite prayer of my father (D. R. Gent, English rugby football international).'

The Revd Rupert Bliss, *retired naval officer, teacher and mathematician*

Within this point of time and space I pray Thee, Lord of Life,
That Thou wilt fortify me with thy Grace,
That what I am and do both here and now
May surely and entirely be
A shining sacrifice of praise to Thee.

Rupert Bliss

A Breton Fisherman's Prayer

Dear God, be good to me,
The sea is so large and our boat is so small.

Anon.

Help us to do your holy will
And praise your name come good or ill.

Rupert Bliss

Rabbi Lionel Blue, *rabbi, author and broadcaster*

-►-►-◄-◄-

The Just Society

Our God and God of our fathers, we thank you for teaching us how to save each other and ourselves, to give and to receive, and to support each other on life's journey. There is no limit to our ascent, for there is no limit to the goodness we can do. There is no joy we cannot have, there is no end to giving. There is no height we cannot attain, for we were created to need each other's love and understanding.

The doors to heaven are open to all mankind. So let us share our blessings and enter in. In the past week we may have denied happiness to others and to ourselves, for selfishness lies in the way, and we can be enemies to our own happiness. Your Sabbath calls us back to the truth. We learn again the way to change hatred into love and banish bitterness. We know again the strength for good that is in our grasp. We see again the purity of our souls and your image shining in us. Blessed are you, Lord, who teaches us to serve each other. Amen.

Written by Lionel Blue for the Jewish Liturgy

Ronald Blythe, *author*

→>-<-

A Suffolk Prayer

We remember before God all those who make our journey here happy and fulfilled, our families and our friends. We name in our hearts those who live a long way from us and we don't often see.

We remember before God all those who are sick in body or in mind, people in hospital, people undergoing difficult treatments.

And we remember before God all those who, for a while, have lost those they loved and are sad.

We remember all prisoners in their isolation and suffering the world over, especially prisoners of conscience.

We thank God for all his mercies to us, for making our lives in this beautiful place, for giving us good food, good homes and good friends. We thank him for the countryside in summer [*season*] and for our gardens and fields. We thank him for the gifts of the spirit, books and music. We thank him for our animals which give us such happiness.

Most of all we thank him for allowing us to come here each week in fellowship and worship as we say the Grace together. . . .

'I wrote this prayer for our Stour Valley churches in Suffolk some years ago and say it at Matins and Evensong every week.'

The Rt. Hon. Betty Boothroyd, *Speaker of the House of Commons*

--+->-<+--

The Queen and Government

Lord, the God of righteousness and truth, grant to our Queen and her Government, to Members of Parliament and all in positions of responsibility, the guidance of your Spirit. May they never lead the nation wrongly through love of power, desire to please or unworthy ideals, but always love righteousness and truth; so may your kingdom come and your name be hallowed; through Jesus Christ our Lord.

Authorship unknown but written for SCM in 1922/23

❡ Each parliamentary day commences with a form of prayer which has not been substantially changed since the seventeenth century (see the choice of Sir Patrick Cormack). Nonetheless there is a more modern prayer, which Betty Boothroyd would commend and which is her choice here.

Dr Alan Borg, *Director of the Victoria and Albert Museum*

-+>-<+-

Aut lego vel scribo, doceo scrutorve sophiam
obsecro celcithronum nocte dieque meum
vescor, poto libens, rithmizians invoco Musas
dormisco stertens: oro deum vigilans.
Conscia mens scelerum deflet peccamina vitae
parcite vos misero, Christe Maria, viro.

(I read or write, I teach or wonder what is truth,
I call upon my God by night and day,
I eat and drink freely, I make my rhymes
And snoring sleep, or vigil keep and pray.
And very ware of all my shames I am;
O Mary, Christ, have mercy on your man.)

Sedulius Scottus (ninth century), translated by Helen Waddell

Mike Brearley, *former captain of the England cricket team*

-+>-<+-

Almighty and most merciful Father; We have erred, and strayed from thy ways like lost sheep. We have followed too much the devices and desires of our own hearts. We have offended against thy holy laws. We have left undone those things which we ought to have done; And we have done those things which we ought not to have done; And there is no health in us. But thou, O Lord, have mercy upon us, miserable offenders. Spare thou them, O God, which confess their faults. Restore thou them that are penitent; According to thy promises declared unto mankind in Christ Jesu our Lord. And grant, O most merciful Father, for his sake; That we may hereafter live a godly, righteous, and sober life, To the glory of thy holy Name. Amen.

Morning Prayer, Book of Common Prayer

'Always read, in a lugubrious voice, at my school assembly by the Deputy Head, a sane, wise, humorous man. It struck me as a sane, wise and truthful prayer.'

Richard Briers, *actor*

Socrates' prayer (from Plato's Phaedrus*)*

Beloved Pan, and all ye other gods
who haunt this place, give me beauty
In the inward soul; and may the outward
And inward man be at one.
May I reckon the wise to be wealthy,
And may I have such a quantity of gold
As a temperate man and he only can
Bear and carry – Anything else?
The prayer I think is enough for me.

Plato (429–349 BC), translated by Benjamin Jowett

¶ Jowett (1817–92), an illustrious Oxford academic, master of Balliol College and Regius Professor of Greek, was for a time deprived of his salary on suspicion of heresy. His translation of this prayer is one of the most sensitive to have been made.

Neil Brown, *Curator of Clocks, the Science Museum*

To every thing there is a season, and a time to every purpose under the heaven:
A time to be born, and a time to die; a time to plant, and a time to pluck up that which is planted;
A time to weep, and a time to laugh; a time to mourn, and a time to dance.

Ecclesiastes 3, verses 1, 2 and 4 (Authorized Version)

Lady Butler of Saffron Walden

->-><-<-

God be in my head, and in my understanding;
God be in my eyes, and in my looking;
God be in my mouth, and in my speaking;
God be in my heart, and in my thinking;
God be at my end, and at my departing.

Sarum Primer (1558)

The Rt. Hon. Lady Justice Butler-Sloss,
Lady Justice of Appeal

->-><-<-

Shew me thy ways, O Lord; teach me thy paths.
Lead me in thy truth, and teach me: for thou art the God of my
    salvation; on thee do I wait all the day.
Remember, O Lord, thy tender mercies and thy loving-kindnesses;
    for they have been ever of old.
Remember not the sins of my youth, nor my transgressions:
    according to thy mercy; remember thou me for thy goodness'
    sake, O Lord.

Psalm 25, verses 4–7 (Authorized Version)

Dominus Jesus sit potus et esus.
(Let the Lord Jesus be food and drink.)

A grace by Martin Luther

John Callear, *veterinary surgeon*

→>‹-

I bring this prayer to you, Lord,
For you alone can give
What one cannot demand but from oneself.

Give me, Lord, what you have left over,
Give me what no one ever asks you for.

I don't ask for rest or quiet,
whether of soul or of body;

I don't ask for wealth.
Nor for success, not even for health perhaps,

That sort of thing you get asked for so much
That you can't have any of it left.

I want insecurity, anxiety,
I want storm and strife
and I want you to give me these once and for all
since I shan't have the courage to ask you for them.

Give me, Lord, what you have left over,
Give me what the others want nothing to do with.

But give me courage too
And strength and faith.

For you alone can give
What one cannot demand but from oneself.

Written in the Western Desert by André Zirnheld, a Free French
member of the SAS and a friend of David Stirling, its leader.
Translated by Professor Alan Steele, Edinburgh University

¶ Alan Hoe, in his biography of David Stirling, says of André Zirnheld, 'He was not cut from the same stuff as the other Frenchmen. Something of a mystic, he had an aura which inspired confidence, devoted to his men, he quickly acquired a high reputation.' The prayer was found on his body after he had been fatally wounded at Sidi Hanneish.

Professor Sir Roy Calne, *transplant surgeon*
(first liver transplant)

→>—<←

Hypothesis
The Creator's Testament to Modern Man

I have given you DNA programmed by evolution through millions of years. It has form, function and instincts derived from your anthropoid ancestors. You have evolved the gift of language and intelligence to possess the ability to reason, to enquire, to have abstract thoughts from which you may experience rich emotions. These blessings bestowed on you are to be used to live in peace with fellow-men, animals, plants and the elements of the earth.

From your ancestors you have inherited the urge to reproduce to preserve your precious DNA. Many of the secrets of nature are now revealed to you by your probing curiosity and rational analysis. This knowledge can be used for good or evil.

The legend of the serpent who gave Eve the fruit of knowledge is a terrible warning; beware not to succumb to the temptations of greed, envy, fanatic hatred and lust for power to dominate others. If you continue to multiply without constraint or consideration of the rest of the world you will swiftly exhaust irreplaceable resources, animal, vegetable and mineral, which will surely lead to the destruction of your DNA and the desolation of the planet.

You will have many hard decisions to make but I have given you the ability to choose. In the spirit of love and compassion towards your fellow-men and all living creatures, animals and plants, use your scientific knowledge to choose and act wisely and to devise ways of sharing without exploitation, to live and let live.

I hope you become *Homo* SAPIENS, the alternative is *Homo* EXTINCTUS.

I wish you well.

Roy Calne

Timothy and Elizabeth Capon,
company director and art gallery guide

→>-<-

Keep me in Thy love
As Thou wouldst that all should be kept in mine.
May everything in this my being be directed to Thy glory
And may I never despair
For I am under Thy hand
And in Thee is all power and goodness.

Dag Hammarskjöld (1905–61)

Those who die in Grace go no further than God,
and God is very near.

The Most Revd the Rt. Hon. Dr George Carey,
Archbishop of Canterbury

→>-<-

Lord Jesus Christ, the Master Carpenter of Nazareth, on a cross of wood and nails you have wrought man's salvation; wield well your tools in this your workshop, so that we who come to you rough-hewn, may by you be fashioned according to your will; for the sake of your tender mercy. Amen.

¶ The origin of this prayer is not clear. One form is used daily in the Christian Industrial Training Centre Schools in Kenya and is attributed to their founder, the Revd Charles Tett, GM (1916–75), whose bravery award was gained as a fire-fighter during the London Blitz; another form is called the Toc H Prayer and is attributed to Hal Pink, about whom no records have been found. A slightly different version, which may be closest to the original, is used regularly in the Iona Community. They may all be derived from an original written by the Revd Arthur Gray of St Francis in the East, Glasgow.

Also chosen by:
Nicholas Bomford, *Headmaster, Harrow School;*
The Revd Norman Shanks, *Leader, Iona Community.*

Rear-Admiral James Carine, *Master of the Worshipful Company of Chartered Secretaries, Secretary of the Arab Horse Society and amateur bookie's runner*

→>—<←

Prayer for the Manx Herring Fishing Fleet

That it may please Thee to give and preserve to our use the kindly fruits of the earth and to restore and continue to us the blessings of the Seas, so as in due time we may enjoy them.

Bishop Wilson, 1708

Jesus, Mary, Joseph, I give you my heart and soul;
Jesus, Mary, Joseph, assist me in my last agony;
Jesus, Mary, Joseph, let me pour forth my soul in peace with you.

'A prayer, now less fashionable, learned from my grandmother.'

¶ The Catholic Liturgy Office confirms that this prayer is translated from the Latin text of the sacrament of Extreme Unction or Last Rites and is one of a series of short prayers used at the point of death (*de expiratione*). The last line is sometimes given as 'Jesus , Mary, Joseph, may I sleep and take my rest in peace with you.'

Brian Carpenter, *postman*

→>—<←

The Lord is my shepherd; I shall not want.
He maketh me to lie down in green pastures: he leadeth me beside
    the still waters.
He restoreth my soul: he leadeth me in the paths of righteousness
for his name's sake.

Psalm 23, verses 1–3 (Authorized Version)

Also chosen by:
Elizabeth Hele, *voluntary worker for CAB and literacy tutoring.*

Deborah Cassidi, *retired doctor*

Jesus, tender Shepherd, hear me,
Bless thy little lamb tonight,
Through the darkness be thou near me,
Keep me safe till morning light.

Through this day thy hand has led me,
And I thank thee for thy care.
Thou hast clothed me, warmed and fed me,
Listen to my evening prayer.

Let my sins be all forgiven,
Bless the friends I love so well;
Take me, when I die, to heaven,
Happy there with thee to dwell.

Mary D. Duncan (1814–40)

'As a child I said this prayer nightly with my mother or grandmother. It has been used thus for four generations of the family.'

Dr Sheila Cassidy, *ex-prisoner of conscience, cancer physician and psychotherapist*

→>-<+

A Prayer for All God's Children

Lord of all hopefulness, Lord of all Joy – we pray for those who have lost hope and courage this day. We pray for the sick: especially those struggling with terminal cancer, AIDS or motor neurone disease. We pray too for prisoners, for refugees, hostages and all who are trapped in unhappy relationships or problems of addiction. We think, too, of the mentally ill: the schizophrenics, the depressed, and those whose personality is crippled by violence, neglect or abuse. We pray especially for those tempted to kill themselves this day, and for those so twisted that they would kill another. More than anything, O Lord, we pray for the children: for the street-children of the developing world, all orphans and refugees, for the hungry, for all who sleep rough on our own streets, and those who are unloved or abused. Open your heart, O Loving God, and fill it with these your children.

¶ Written by Sheila Cassidy in response to our request, August 1997.

Fiona Castle, *leader of 'Care for the Family'*

→>-<+

Teach me your ways, O Lord my God,
And I will walk in your truth;
Give me a totally undivided heart;
Cleanse me, Lord, I pray;
Remove from me all that is
standing in the way of your love.

Eugene Greco

¶ Used by Roy and Fiona at Christmas 1992 in a television programme and her constant prayer since that time.

(Copyright © 1990 Kingsway's Thankyou Music)

Beth Chatto, *gardener and writer*

→>-<←

Prayer for Rain

God, make it rain!
Loose the soft silver passion of the rain!
Send swiftly from above
This clear token of Thy love.
Make it rain!

Deck the bushes and the trees
With the tassels of the rain.
Make the brooks pound to the seas
And the earth shine young again.
God of passion, send the rain!

Oh, restore our ancient worth
With Thy rain!
Ease the heartache of the earth;
Sap the grain.
Fill the valleys and the dales
With Thy silver slanting gales;
And through England and wild Wales
Send the rain!

Lord, restore us to Thy will
With the rain!
Soak the valley, drench the hill,
Drown the stain;
Smite the mountain's withered hips,
Wash the rouge from sunset's lips,
Fill the sky with singing ships.
Send the rain!

Herbert E. Palmer

Lieutenant-Commander Mike Cheshire, *Captain of HMS Victory*

May the great God, whom I worship, grant to my Country and for the benefit of Europe in general, a great and glorious victory: and may no misconduct, in any one, tarnish it: and may humanity after victory be the predominant feature in the British Fleet.

For myself individually, I commit my life to Him who made me and may His blessing light upon my endeavours for serving my Country faithfully.

To Him I resign myself and the just cause which is entrusted to me to defend. AMEN AMEN AMEN.

Horatio Nelson (1758–1805)

❡ Written on the morning of 21 October 1805, the combined fleets of France and Spain being then in sight.

Anthony Clothier, *shoemaker and forester*

-+->-<-+-

On Marriage

Never marry but for love; but see that thou lovest what is lovely. He that minds a body and not a soul has not the better part of that relation and will consequently want the noblest comfort of a married life.

Between a man and his wife nothing ought to rule but love. As love ought to bring them together so it is the best way to keep them well together.

A husband and wife that love and value one another show their children that they should do so too. Others visibly lose their authority in their families by their contempt of one another, and teach their children to be unnatural by their own examples.

Let not enjoyment lessen, but augment affection; it being the basest of passions to like, when we have not, what we slight when we possess. Here it is we ought to search out our pleasure of an enduring nature; sickness, poverty, or disgrace being not able to shake it, because it is not under the moving influences of worldly contingencies.

Nothing can be more entire and without reserve, nothing more zealous, affectionate and sincere, nothing more contented and constant than such a couple, nor no greater temporal felicity than to be one of them.

William Penn (1644–1718)

'Not exactly a prayer but I have found parts of it very helpful.'

John Coldebank, *iron foundry worker, Lancashire*

-+>-+>-<+-

All things bright and beautiful,
All creatures great and small,
All things wise and wonderful,
The Lord God made them all.

He gave us eyes to see them,
And lips that we might tell
How great is God Almighty,
Who has made all things well.

Mrs C. F. Alexander (1818–95)

Also chosen by:
Mary Heck, *Somerset farmhouse cider-maker.*

Richard Constable, *artist, great-grandson of John Constable*

-+>-<+-

Approach all things with open mind;
All have gifts to which we're blind;
Be sensitive to others' cries;
Others too are also wise.

Richard Constable

'It is hardly a prayer but the sentiment behind it is prayerful – that we listen to others who have a right to their opinions and are not necessarily wrong because they disagree with us!'

John Conteh, *World Light Heavyweight Boxing Champion 1974*

If you live in the shelter of Elyon and make your home in the
 shadow of Shaddai,
you can say to Yahweh, 'My refuge and my fortress, my God in
 whom I trust!'

Psalm 91, verses 1 and 2 (The Jerusalem Translation of the Bible, used by many,
including Catholic and Protestant denominations and the Jehovah's Witnesses)

'Given to me by a Jehovah's Witness one morning when I was in trouble.'

Jonathan Cooke, *clerk, The Leathersellers' Company*

Bless, O Lord, before we dine,
Each dish of food, each glass of wine
And Bless our Hearts that we may be
Aware of what we owe to Thee.

Nineteenth-century Leathersellers' Company anthology

Henry Cooper, *Heavyweight Boxing Champion, European and British titles 1959–70*

Life without faith is an arid business.

Attributed to Sir Noel Coward

'A favourite quotation of mine.'

¶ Though this saying is not recorded in the archives, both Joan Hirst (assistant to
Lorn Loraine) and Graham Payn, lifelong friend of Coward's, agree that it might
very well have been one of his spontaneous comments.

Jilly Cooper, *author*

->-<-

Prayer for an adopted child

Not flesh of my flesh
nor bone of my bone
but still, miraculous,
my own.
Never forget
for a single minute,
you didn't grow under my heart
but in it.

Anon.

'The adoption poem is a beautiful poem. It is anonymous and nobody seems to know who wrote it. I think it is a prayer although it is a poem, because it is so beautiful.'

From *The Rime of the Ancient Mariner*

Beyond the shadow of the ship,
I watched the water-snakes:
They moved in tracks of shining white,
And when they reared, the elfish light
Fell off in hoary flakes.

Within the shadow of the ship
I watched their rich attire:
Blue, glossy green, and velvet black,
They coiled and swam; and every track
Was a flash of golden fire.

O happy living things! no tongue
Their beauty might declare:
A spring of love gushed from my heart,
And I blessed them unaware:
Sure my kind saint took pity on me,
And I blessed them unaware.

The self-same moment I could pray;
And from my neck so free
The Albatross fell off, and sank
Like lead into the sea.

Samuel Taylor Coleridge (1772–1834)

'I love these verses of the *Ancient Mariner* which aren't really a prayer, but to me seem to be a prayer to say we should look after all creatures great and small. It is the most poignant moment in the *Ancient Mariner*, when the Mariner, cursed for his crime against Creation, that of killing the Albatross, suddenly, without thinking, blesses the water snakes for their beauty. Immediately the Albatross falls from his neck.'

Sir Patrick Cormack, *MP*

Almighty God, by whom alone Kings reign and Princes decree justice, and from whom alone cometh all counsel, wisdom and understanding; we Thine unworthy servants here gathered together in Thy name do most humbly beseech Thee to send down Thy heavenly wisdom from above, to direct and guide us in all our consultations: And grant that, we having Thy fear always before our eyes, and laying aside all private interests, prejudices and partial affections, the result of all our counsels may be to the glory of Thy blessed Name, the maintenance of true Religion and justice, the safety, honour and happiness of the Queen, the publick wealth, peace and tranquillity of the Realm, and the uniting and knitting together of the hearts of all persons and estates within the same, in true Christian Love and Charity one towards another.

Authorship unknown but used, on a daily basis, continuously since the
seventeenth century

¶ Official Daily Prayer for Parliament, used by the Speaker's Chaplain at the commencement of each day's business. The first Speaker's Chaplain was appointed in 1659. The Speaker does not take the Chair, the Clerks remain outside the Chamber, and strangers are excluded from the Public Galleries until prayers are finished.

Marshal of the Royal Air Force Lord Craig of Radley

O Lord my Master, prepare me to receive Thee in this Holy Sacrament. Then come in all Thy might; let Thy strength make me strong, let Thy purity make me pure, let Thy gentleness make me kind, that as Thy fellow-worker I may help to make this world a better place, according to Thy will, who art God for ever and ever. Amen.

'Given to me in a very small prayer book by my headmaster at my confirmation and used by me from memory ever since.'

¶ This prayer is probably by Herbert Tomkinson, who wrote the preface to the small book referred to (*My Prayer Book*).

Martin Cross, *oarsman, Olympic Gold Medallist*

Jesus, I have spent so much time training for this race
that sometimes it has been difficult to find a
place for You in my life.
But help me to make each stroke a prayer for You,
accepting victory with humility, defeat with magnanimity,
so that through my words and deeds
I may glorify You and help others
to walk in the light of Your presence.

Martin Cross

Mary Crossley, *carpet manufacturer, Halifax*

→►◄←

O God, early in the morning I cry to you. Help me to pray and to concentrate my thoughts on you: I cannot do this alone.

In me there is darkness. But with you there is light; I am lonely, but you do not leave me; I am feeble in heart, but with you there is help; I am restless, but with you there is peace. In me there is bitterness, but with you there is patience; I do not understand your ways, but you know the way for me.

Restore me to liberty, and enable me so to live now that I may answer before you and before men. Lord, whatever this day may bring, your name be praised. Amen.

Dietrich Bonhoeffer, 1906–45 (written in prison while he was awaiting execution)

'Bonhoeffer was hanged in Flossenburg concentration camp on 9 April 1945. A week later the camp was liberated by the Allies.'

His Eminence Cardinal Cahal Daly, *former Archbishop of Armagh*

Prayer of Abandonment

Father,
I abandon myself into your hands;
do with me what you will.
Whatever you may do I thank you:
I am ready for all, I accept all.

Let only your will be done in me,
and in all your creatures.
I wish nothing more than this, O Lord.

Into your hands I commend my soul:
I offer it to you
with all the love of my heart,
for I do love you, Lord,
and so I need to give myself,s
to surrender myself into your hands,
without reserve,
and with boundless confidence,
because you are my Father.

Charles de Foucauld (1858–1916), translated by Cardinal Daly

¶ Charles de Foucauld initially led a dissipated life but after his military service (distinguished by its bravery) in the Sahara, this changed. He became a Trappist hermit in the Sahara, respected by and serving the Tuareg and other Muslim desert tribes. Tragically, he was murdered by a member of a fanatical sect. Soon beatified, his life inspired the founding of both the Little Brothers and Little Sisters of Jesus.

Also chosen by:
Lady Moyra Campbell, *Regional Trustee for the NSPCC, Northern Ireland.*

Patrick Darling, *Major, the Light Dragoons, 1st Reconnaissance Brigade*

➤➤◄◄

Sarajevo

Sometimes in a dream I go to Sarajevo, that beautiful town,
To drink rakija with friends before the dawn.
Once more the winds of happiness, scented and young,
Roll her white sandals Marijan Dvor along.

Only in my dreams do I carry flowers to the maternity clinic
Where my sons, the babies of Sarajevo, were born,
Young fathers miming in the joy of spring
Kissing their hands to the women showing pale like amoeba.

I loved the shadow of the white birch trees above the grave of my
    parents
Where now I see the bird with the sliced human entrails.
Oh God, let me go through each beautiful city
But don't let me go to Sarajevo even in dream.

Dejan Gutalj

'These verses from a poem by a Serb soldier in the trenches overlooking Sarajevo were sent to me by two Serbian friends, Lana and Ceca, from Pale when I left after my second stint in Bosnia. The poem was translated by Major Pickles and edited by Lana and Ceca, who also sent me the Lord's Prayer in Serbo-Croat.

'While I was in Bosnia I attended church with the Croats. There was never more than standing room and services were recited. In Tomislavgrad the church was boarded up against artillery fire and a power cut on Christmas Eve meant that the service was conducted by the light of a few candles. In Sarajevo, my memory is of the intense cold after the services. In Zepce I was given a breakfast of smoked ham and boiled eggs on Easter Sunday. I felt so humble. These people had lost everything and yet shared what little they had with a stranger.

'I pray that God will strengthen the good that is to be found in the individuals in Bosnia, amongst the three factions, and help them to find room in their hearts to forgive the past and build the future.'

The Lord's Prayer in Serbo-Croat

Oče nas, koji jesi na nebesima,
sveti se ime tvoje,
dodji kraljevstvo tvoje,
budi volja tvoja kako na nebu tako i na zemlji.
Kruh nas svagdanji daj nam danas.
I otpusti nam duge naše
kako I mi otpuštamo dunicima našim.
I ne uvedi nas u napast,
nego izbavi nas od zla.

Edward Darwin,
psychotherapist, grandson of Charles Darwin

→>–<←

Look, Father, look on his anointed face,
and only look on us as found in him;
Look not on our misusings of thy grace,
our prayers so languid, and our faith so dim;
For lo! between our sins and their reward
We set the passion of thy son Our Lord.

From 'And now, O Father' by William Bright (1824–1901)

'Used in preparation for communion.'

Dame Judi Dench, *actress*

→>–<←

O Lord! Thou knowest how busy I must be this day: If I forget Thee do not thou forget me.

Prayer of Sir Jacob Astley (1579–1652) before the battle of Edgehill on 13 October 1642, found in Sir Philip Warwick's memoirs, 1701

Also chosen by:
Robert Dunning, *county historian;*
Adam Gosling, *World champion, Etchell Racing Dinghies 1996;*
John Julius Norwich, *author and broadcaster;*
Ernest Rea, *Head of Religious Broadcasting at the BBC;*
Dame Barbara Shenfield, *former Chairman at the WRVS;*
and **Robert Walrond**, *Somerset sheep farmer, who wrote from his farm, 'It has been hectic this week, we are in the middle of lambing. This prayer gives me reassurance that in these busy periods, God is always there, finding time for me.'*

Dudley Doust, *cricket commentator and author*

From *Pied Beauty*

Glory be to God for dappled things –
For skies of couple-colour as a brinded cow;
For rose-moles all in stipple upon trout that swim;
Fresh-firecoal chestnut-falls; finches' wings;
Landscape plotted and pieced – fold, fallow, and plough;
And, all trades, their gear and tackle and trim.

Gerard Manley Hopkins (1844–1889)

'You need not be religious to be captured by the spiritual joy and poetic fun expressed by Hopkins.'

Also chosen by:
Rebecca John, *botanical artist, granddaughter of Augustus John.*

Though I am different from you,
We were born involved
In one another.

Tao Ch'ien

William Dowling, *homeless,* Big Issue *seller*

O Lord, grant me to greet the coming day in peace. Help me in all things to rely upon thy holy will. In every hour of the day reveal thy will to me. Bless my dealings with all who surround me. Teach me to treat all that comes to me throughout the day with peace of soul, and with firm conviction that thy will governs all. In all my deeds and words guide my thoughts and feelings. In unforeseen events let me not forget that all are sent by thee. Teach me to act firmly and wisely, without embittering and embarrassing others. Give me strength to bear the fatigue of the coming day with all that it shall bring. Direct my will, teach me to pray, pray thou thyself in me.

Metropolitan Philaret of Moscow (1782–1867)

Sir John Drinkwater, *QC, barrister*

Benedic, Domine, nos et haec tua dona quae de bonitate tua sumpturi sumus.
(Bless, O God, us and these Thy gifts which, through Thy bounty, we are about to receive.)

'Before being called to the bar, by the Inner Temple, I found myself on circuit as a Judge's Marshal to three Judges, all from Gray's Inn, who liked to have it said daily.'

❡ Usually said at Gray's Inn, before dinner in Hall, by the Treasurer, this Grace was first recorded in 1711 but probably dates to pre-Reformation days.

Thank God.

'My favourite Grace, used much at sea and rather like myself, short and broad.'

John Dunford, *Headmaster of Durham Johnston Comprehensive School, Durham*

Go forth into the world in peace;
be of good courage;
hold fast that which is good;
render to no man evil for evil;
strengthen the faint-hearted;
support the weak; help the afflicted;
honour all men; love and serve the Lord;
rejoicing in the power of the Holy Spirit;
and the blessing of God Almighty,
the Father, the Son and the Holy Ghost be upon you
and remain with you for ever.

The Prayer Book, as proposed in 1928 (Confirmation Blessing)

'This prayer is used at the Assembly held at the end of every year for those who are leaving school.'

Neil Durden-Smith, *company director, Lord's Taverner*

→>·<←

The Ship

What is dying?
I am standing on the sea shore,
a ship sails in the morning breeze
and starts for the ocean.
She is an object of beauty
and I stand watching her
till at last she fades
on the horizon
and someone at my side says:
'She is gone.'
Gone! Where?
Gone from my sight – that is all.
She is just as large in the masts, hull and spars
as she was when I saw her,
and just as able to bear her load of living
freight to its destination.
The diminished size and total loss of sight is in me,
not in her,
and just at the moment when someone at my side says,
'She is gone'
there are others who are watching her coming,
and other voices take up a glad shout:
'There she comes!'
– and that is dying.

Bishop Brent (1862–1926)

Also chosen by:
Judith Chalmers, *broadcaster.*

Lady Eames, *Mothers' Union worldwide president*

-+>-<+-

O God, we pray for all who have the privilege and responsibility of nurturing the children of this world. May they be conscious of the task entrusted to them to enable each child to grow and develop in mind, in body and in spirit. May they encourage each young person to find the gifts You have given them and work so that every home is touched by Christ.

Christine Eames

'The Mothers' Union is a Christian organization concerned with the well-being of families worldwide. It has three-quarters of a million members who promote their aims both by prayer and action.'

The Most Revd the Rt. Hon. Lord Eames, *Archbishop of Armagh*

-+>-<+-

Almighty and most merciful God, grant me something of Your peace that when I am rushed and pressurized by demands and events I may never forget You or lose sight of your love for all mankind. In that peace grant me the wisdom to know what I should leave for others to do. Through Jesus Christ our Lord. Amen.

R. H. A. Eames

❡ A prayer of his own which he has used on many occasions.

Jean Edwards, *grandmother*

->><-

May the roads rise to meet you, may the wind be always at your back, may the sun shine warm upon your face, the rains fall soft upon your fields and until we meet again may God hold you in the hollow of His hand.

An Irish blessing

Also chosen by:
William Montgomery, *fine arts expert and farmer, and his wife,* **Daphne**.

Valerie Eliot, *widow of T. S. Eliot*

->><-

O Light Invisible, we praise Thee!
Too bright for mortal vision.
O Greater Light, we praise Thee for the less;
The eastern light our spires touch at morning,
The light that slants upon our western doors at evening,
The twilight over stagnant pools at batflight,
Moon light and star light, owl and moth light,
Glow-worm glowlight on a grassblade.
O Light Invisible, we worship Thee!

We thank Thee for the lights that we have kindled,
The light of altar and of sanctuary;
Small lights of those who meditate at midnight
And lights directed through the coloured panes of windows
And light reflected from the polished stone,
The gilded carven wood, the coloured fresco.
Our gaze is submarine, our eyes look upward
And see the light that fractures through unquiet water.
We see the light but see not whence it comes.
O Light Invisible, we glorify Thee!

From 'The Rock', by T. S. Eliot (1888–1965)

Also chosen by:
Revd Stephen Connor, *team vicar.*

Peter and Penny Ellis, *retired barrister and wife*

-+->-<-+-

The Rune of Saint Patrick

At Tara today in this fateful hour
I place all Heaven with its power
and the sun with its brightness,
and the snow with its whiteness,
and fire with all the strength it hath,
and lightning with its rapid wrath,
and the winds with their swiftness along their path,

and the sea with its deepness,
and the rocks with their steepness,
and the earth with its starkness:
   all these I place,
    by God's almighty help and grace
between myself and the powers of darkness.

James Clarence Mangan (1803–49)

Richard Field, *Master Cutler, The Company of Cutlers in Hallamshire, Sheffield*

-+->-<-+-

Lord, bless this food upon these dishes,
As Thou didst bless the loaves and fishes.
And like the sugar in our tea,
May all of us be stirred by thee.

From Carolyn Martin, *A Book of Graces*

'Life can sometimes feel far too serious, but this grace gives me joy.'

Sir Ranulph Fiennes, *explorer*

-+->-<-+-

Always a little further, pilgrim.

Dick Francis, *author*

May I deal with honour.
May I act with courage.
May I achieve humility.

Dick Francis

¶ Dick Francis says that the words for this prayer came immediately to him. They feature among the possessions of one of his heroes in *Straight*.

Douglas Fraser, *schoolboy from Somerset*

Dear God,
Thank you for the new life in the Spring Time with all the lambs and all the little snowdrops.

Douglas Fraser (aged 9)

Fiona Fraser, *leader of an inter-faith group*

✦

O Father, give the spirit power to climb
to the fountain of all light, and be purified.
Break through the mists of earth, the weight of the clod,
Shine forth in splendour, Thou that art calm weather,
And quiet resting place for the faithful souls.
To see Thee is the end and the beginning,
Thou carriest us, and Thou dost go before,
Thou art the journey, and the journey's end.

Boethius (*c*.480–*c*.524)

Pain That Heals

Let the healing grace of your love, O Lord, so transform me that I may play my part in the transfiguration of the world from a place of suffering, death and corruption to a realm of infinite light, joy and love. Make me so obedient to your spirit that my life may become a place of living prayer, and a witness to your unfailing presence.

Martin Israel

Julian Freeman-Attwood, *Himalayan and Antarctic mountaineer*

Out of the gloom
A voice said unto me,
'Smile and be happy,
Things could be worse.'
So I smiled and was happy
And, behold, things did get worse.

Unknown source

'I am, from time to time, in less than comfortable situations (as in storms at night) and the thought of this prayer or poem has always made me smile.'

Annette Gage, *pancake-maker*

When you are joyous, look deep into your heart and you shall find it is only that which has given you sorrow that is giving you joy. When you are sorrowful, look again in your heart, and you shall see that in truth you are weeping for that which has been your delight.

From *The Prophet* by Kahlil Gibran (1883–1931)

James Galway, *flautist*

→>-<-

In the Morning

O God, our Father, deliver us this day from all that would keep us from serving Thee and from serving our fellowmen as we ought.

Deliver us from all coldness of heart; and grant that neither our hand nor our heart may ever remain shut to the appeal of someone's need.

Deliver us from all weakness of will; from the indecision which cannot make up its mind; from the irresolution which cannot abide by a decision once it is made; from the inability to say No to the tempting voices which come to us from inside and from outside.

Deliver us from all failure in endeavour; from being too easily discouraged; from giving up and giving in too soon; from allowing any task to defeat us, because it is difficult.

Grant unto us this day the love which is generous in help; the determination which is steadfast in decision; the perseverance which is enduring unto the end; through Jesus Christ our Lord.

William Barclay

'Because of the very personal relationship I have with God my prayers are never the same but I have chosen almost at random from *The Plain Man's Book of Prayer.*'

John Garrett, *borough councillor,*
Cambridge rowing Blue, and Olympic oarsman

→>–<←

Everybody can be great. Because anybody can serve. You don't have to have a college degree to serve. You don't have to make your subject and your verb agree to serve. You don't have to know Einstein's Theory of Relativity to serve. You don't have to know the second theorem of thermo-dynamics in physics to serve. You only need a heart full of grace. A soul generated by love.

The Revd Martin Luther King, Jr (1926–68)

Eddie George, *Governor of the Bank of England*

→>–<←

Teach us, good Lord,
to serve Thee as Thou deservest;
to give and not to count the cost;
to fight and not to heed the wounds;
to toil and not to seek for rest;
to labour and not to ask for any reward
save that of knowing that we do Thy will.

St Ignatius Loyola (1491–1556)

Also chosen by:
John Dunford, *comprehensive school headmaster;*
David Baddams, *Harrier jet pilot, who said, 'This was our school prayer at Westminster School, Adelaide, Australia, and expressed some of the best qualities to try to follow.'*

Peter George, *friend*

✦✦✦

I don't want to be the Christ, dear Lord.
I'd rather be myself and feel free.
You keep on calling me, and, overawed,
I beg you, saying 'Dear Lord, don't choose me.
I can't do miracles, or prophesy.
I'm weak and weary, sick and soaked in sin.'
Yet day and night I hear the same reply,
'I love you and I want you to begin.'
    O Lord, I feel you love me even though
    You tell me things I do not want to know.

From a prayer by David Caccia (died 15 December 1983)

I do not know how to pray but I do say, 'Please help Mum to turn
me.'

Paul Muncey (a quadriplegic)

Helen Gibbins, *youth worker*

✦✦✦

God Be with You with God

No prayer unanswered is,
If He say 'yes', 'tis well,
Or He answer 'wait',
Rest suppliant at his gate.
He never answers 'no',
But that in time,
Some richer fuller gift is thine.

R. E. Cleeve

Christopher Gibbs, *art dealer*

✦

O Lord Jesus, pray in us.
Dwell in us and we in Thee.
Unite us with Thyself so that our prayers
may become Thy prayers
and Thy prayers our prayers.
Make us to love Thee for Thine own sake
and not for what we hope from Thee.
Teach us to love as Thou lovest. Amen.

Elizabeth Basset

Ruth Gledhill, *Religion Correspondent,* The Times

✦

Lord, make me an instrument of your peace.
Where there is hatred let me sow love,
Where there is injury, pardon;
Where there is doubt, faith;
Where there is despair, hope;
Where there is darkness, light;
Where there is sadness, joy.
O divine Master, grant that I may not so much seek
To be consoled, as to console,
To be understood, as to understand,
To be loved, as to love;
For it is in giving that we receive;
It is in pardoning that we are pardoned;
It is in dying that we are born to eternal life. Amen.

Attributed to St Francis of Assisi, this prayer first appeared in print in the 1920s

'I use this prayer every morning and night or even in the car or Tube, also when frustrated by a provocative caller, a piece of meaningless liturgy or a failure to succeed. It controls my quick temper and puts life in perspective.'

Also chosen by:
Countess Mountbatten; **John Tupper,** *retired aviator; and* **John Tydeman,** *former Director of Drama, BBC Radio 4.*

The Hon. Sir David Gore-Booth, *British High Commissioner, New Delhi*

➤➤◄◄

For Tolerance

Father of all men, free us from every prejudice born of hate and fear and kept alive by ignorance and pride. Open our hearts and minds to new friendships and new contributions of the spirit from races and cultures, religions and classes other than our own.

Enrich us by the great thoughts and experiences of all peoples and countries. With all thy children on earth make us sharers of thine abundant life and workers together in thy kingdom of love and peace.

G. A. Cleveland Shrigley

'This prayer comes from a book given to my wife by her father many years ago. It is relevant to my service in India and I like its plea for tolerance.'

John Gould, *Cheddar cheese maker*

➤➤◄◄

Jesus, Friend of little children,
Be a friend to me;
Take my hand, and ever keep me
Close to thee.

Walther J. Mathams (1853–1931)

General Sir Michael Gow, *author and soldier, GOC Scotland and Governor of Edinburgh Castle 1979–80*

Almighty God, whose blessed Son did say unto St Andrew 'Follow Me', grant that the Scots Guards, who wear the cross of Thy Holy Apostle, may follow Thy Son with impunity; be made stronger in brotherhood and fierce against all enemies of our Saviour; ever going forward under the leadership of Him, who by the hard and painful way of the Cross, won high conquest and great glory, even Jesus Christ our Lord. Amen.

D. H. Whiteford

'This is the Regimental Collect of the Scots Guards, whose badge is St Andrew's Cross. Their motto, shared with the Order of the Thistle, is "Nemo me impune lacessit" – "Nobody touches me with impunity", or, as King George V is reputed to have said, "Beware of provoking the Scots Guards".'

Lucinda Green, *Olympic equestrian and author*

Look up and laugh and live.

'These words were a support at a time of bereavement. They kept me going and still do at a bad time.'

❡ The full text of a prayer from which these words may come is:

I would be true for there are those who trust me;
I would be pure for there are those who care;
I would be brave for there is much to suffer;
I would be strong for there is much to dare;
I would be friend of all, the foe, the friendless;
I would be giving and forget the gift;
I would be humble for I know my weakness;
I would look up and love and laugh and live.

From a text by Harold Arnold Walter and J. T. Wenham

The Rt. Hon. the Earl Haig, *painter*

→>-<-

The kiss of the sun for pardon,
　The song of the birds for mirth,
One is nearer God's Heart in a garden
　Than anywhere else on earth.

Dorothy Frances Gurney (1858–1932)

'This is from a stone placed in his garden by my father. It is a kind of celebratory prayer. If you cannot be happy in a garden there might be something wrong.'

Robin Hanbury-Tenison, *traveller, writer, Chief Executive of the British Field Sports Society*

→>-<-

May the roof above never fall in,
May we below never fall out.

An Irish grace

Sir John Harvey-Jones, *industrialist*

→>-<-

O Trinity of love and power,
Our brethren shield in danger's hour;
From rock and tempest, fire and foe,
Protect them wheresoe'er they go;
And ever let there rise to Thee
Glad hymns of praise from land and sea.

From the Mariners' Hymn, 'Eternal father, strong to save' by William Whiting
(1825–78)

'The prayer has long had a particular meaning for me, different parts being suitable for different sections of life.'

Michael Hawke, *hospice director*

-->--<--

I asked God for strength that I might achieve,
I was made weak that I might learn humbly to obey;
I asked for health that I might do greater things,
I was given infirmity that I might do better things;
I asked for riches that I might be happy,
I was given poverty that I might be wise;
I asked for power that I might have the praise of men,
I was given weakness that I might feel the need of God;
I got nothing that I asked for,
But everything I hoped for;
I am among all men most richly blessed.

Attributed to an American Confederate soldier and also to Henry Viscadi

Also chosen by:
Selina Marcon, *lay pastor.*

Paddy Heazell, *retired prep school headmaster*

->->-<-<-

Green Blackboards

The school is up to date.
Proudly the principal tells of all the improvements.
The finest discovery, Lord, is the green blackboard.
The scientists have studied long, they have made experiments:
We know now that green is the ideal colour, that it doesn't tire the
    eyes, that it is quieting and relaxing.

It has occurred to me, Lord, that you didn't wait so long to paint the
    trees and meadows green.
Your research laboratories were efficient, and in order not to tire us,
    you perfected a number of shades of green for your modern
    meadows.
And so the 'finds' of men consist in discovering what you have
    known from time immemorial.

Thank you, Lord, for being the good Father who gives his children
    the joy of discovering by themselves the treasures of his
    intelligence and love,
But keep us from believing that – by ourselves – we have invented
    anything at all.

Michel Quoist, translated by A. M. de Commaile and A. M. Forsyth

Paul Heim, *barrister*

+>-<+

Let Man Remember

Let man remember all the days of his life
He moves at the grave's request.
He goes a little journey every day
And thinks he is at rest;
Like someone lying on board a ship
Which flies at the wind's behest

Moses ibn Ezra (*c*.1055–*c*.1137)

¶ Moses ibn Ezra, a philosopher, Biblical commentator, poet and astronomer, was probably a native of Granada. He survived both the persecution of the Jews in 1066 and the destruction of the city by Berbers in 1090. He travelled widely in Europe, including London. This version was translated by David Goldstein (1933–81), rabbi and curator of Hebrew Books and Manuscripts at the British Library.

Derek Hill, *artist, Tate Gallery exhibitor, previous Director of Art at the British School at Rome*

->>-<+-

Peace was all I ever asked,
'Twas all that was denied;
The angels of the Lord, it seemed,
Fought on the other side.

'My own epitaph!'

Edward (Ted) Hollands, *postman (Higher Grade)*

->>-<+-

Behold, how good and how pleasant it is for brethren to dwell together in unity!
[It is] as the dew that descended upon the mountains of Zion: for there the Lord commanded the blessing, even life for evermore.

Psalm 133, verses 1 and 3 (Authorized Version)

The Rt. Hon. the Earl of Home, *banker*

✦

Give me
A pure heart
That I may see thee,
A humble heart
That I may hear thee,
A heart of love
That I may serve thee,
A heart of faith
That I may abide in thee.

From *Vägmärken* (Markings) by Dag Hammarskjöld (1905–61)

❡ A prayer used at the Earl's father's memorial service in Westminster Abbey in 1996.

Also chosen by:
Revd Ivor Hughes, *rector and Rotarian.*

Nigel Hopkins, *refuse lorry driver*

✦

Abide with me; fast falls the eventide;
The darkness deepens; Lord, with me abide;
When other helpers fail, and comforts flee,
Help of the helpless, O abide with me.

Henry F. Lyte (1793–1847)

Also chosen by:
Margery Wright, *wife of retired thatcher.*

Sheelah Horsfield, *gardener*

→>─<─

Celtic Blessing from the Iona Community

Deep peace of the running wave to you,
deep peace of the flowing air to you,
deep peace of the quiet earth to you,
deep peace of the shining stars to you,
deep peace of the Son of peace to you.

Source unknown (early Scottish)

Come Holy Dove

When I feel alone Your Presence is ever with me.
Come Holy Dove, cover with love.
When I feel weak your strength will seek me.
Come Holy Dove, cover with love.

Spirit be about my head,
Spirit peace around me shed,
Spirit light about my way,
Spirit guardian night and day.

Come Holy Dove,
Cover with love.

David Adam

His Eminence Cardinal Basil Hume, *Archbishop of Westminster*

→>‹←

Since death must be my ending
In that dread hour of need,
My friendless cause befriending,
Lord, to my rescue speed;
Thyself, dear Jesus, trace me
That passage to the grave,
And from thy Cross embrace me
With arms outstretched to save.

A verse from the thirteenth-century hymn, 'O sacred head ill-usèd', translated by
Ronald Knox (1888–1957)

'I love those words and when I sing that hymn, especially in Holy Week, I find it gives me much hope.'

Cecily Ilbert, *artist and teacher*

→>‹←

Coistrig Mathar

Be the great God between thy two shoulders,
To protect thee in thy going and in thy coming,
Be the Son of Mary Virgin near thine heart,
And be the perfect Spirit upon thee pouring,–
Oh, the perfect Spirit upon thee pouring!

Collected and translated by Alexander Carmichael (1832–1912)

❡ Dr Carmichael wrote in *Carmina Gadelica,* 'These words are whispered by mothers into the ears of sons and daughters when leaving their homes in the Outer Isles.'

Brian Irvine, *football player (Aberdeen F.C.)*

⇥⇤

Because He Lives

God sent His Son, they called Him Jesus;
He came to love, heal and forgive;
He lived and died to buy my pardon,
an empty grave is there to prove my Saviour lives.

Because He lives I can face tomorrow;
because He lives all fear is gone;
because I know He holds the future,
and life is worth the living
　　　　just because He lives.

William J. Gaither (copyright © 1971 Kingsway's Thankyou Music)

Mary Irwin, *widow of Col. John Irwin, of* Apollo XV,
*whose 'moon walks' in the Hadley-Apennines area of the
Moon totalled over 18 hours*

⸺>⸺<⸺

High Flight

Oh! I have slipped the surly bonds of earth
And danced the skies on laughter-silvered wings;
Sunward I've climbed, and joined the tumbling mirth
Of sun-split clouds … and done a hundred things
You have not dreamed of … wheeled and soared and swung
High in the sunlit silence. Hov'ring there
I've chased the shouting wind along, and flung
My eager craft through footless hall of air.

Up, up the long, delirious, burning blue
I've topped the wind-swept heights with easy grace
Where never lark, nor even eagle flew …
And, while with silent lifting mind I've trod
The high untrespassed sanctity of space,
Put out my hand and touched the face of God.

John Gillespie Magee, Jr (1922–41)

❡ J. G. Magee, an American, was born of missionary parents in Shanghai
and educated at Rugby School. He won a scholarship to Yale but, feeling he
must aid the cause of freedom, enlisted in the Spitfire Squadron of the
Royal Canadian Air Force. He died on active service on 11 December 1941.
This sonnet, composed three months before his death, was scribbled on the
back of a letter to his mother in Washington.

Saeed Jaffrey, *actor*

→>-<+-

Bismillah-ir-Rehmaan-ur-Raheem. Ya Ali Mooshkil-Koosha,
muddud. Ya Ali muddud, Ya Ali, muddud.
(In the name of God, the compassionate, the merciful. O Ali, solver
of difficulties, help. O Ali help. O Ali help.)

'Taught me by my father and mother, this Urdu prayer has helped me and
those close to me on countless occasions. The opening is that of the Quran,
the rest refers to Hazrat Ali, the Prophet's son-in-law who, in Islam, is
referred to as Mooshkil-Koosha, the one who helps you out of difficulties.'

Nigel James, milkman

→>-<+-

If I could build a stairway,
Our memories are a lane,
I'd walk right up to heaven,
And then be home again!

Nigel James

Baroness James of Holland Park (P. D. James), *author*

→>-<+-

O Lord, who hast taught us that all our doings without charity are
nothing worth; Send thy Holy Ghost, and pour into our hearts that
most excellent gift of charity, the very bond of peace and of all
virtues, without which whosoever liveth is counted dead before
thee: Grant this for thine only Son Jesus Christ's sake. Amen.

Collect for the Sunday called Quinquagesima, Book of Common Prayer

'When I was at school in Ludlow, we were taught the Collect for each
Sunday, so that these prayers, so pregnant with meaning, entered my con-
sciousness early, becoming part of my religious and literary heritage. This
Collect, which has a medieval origin, is a favourite of mine and one of
Cranmer's most beautiful prayers.'

Sir Antony Jay, *scriptwriter and author*

→>—<←

Easter Hymn

If in that Syrian garden, ages slain,
You sleep, and know not you are dead in vain,
Nor even in dreams behold how dark and bright
Ascends in smoke and fire by day and night
The hate you died to quench and could but fan,
Sleep well and see no morning, son of man.

But if, the grave rent and the stone rolled by,
At the right hand of majesty on high
You sit, and sitting so remember yet
Your tears, your agony and bloody sweat,
Your cross and passion and the life you gave,
Bow hither out of heaven and see and save.

A. E. Housman (1859–1936)

'Did A. E. Housman believe in God? This is the best evidence in support of those who say he did.'

From ghoulies and ghosties and long leggety beasties
And things that go bump in the night,
    Good Lord, deliver us!

Cornish prayer

Prayer for a Very New Angel

God, God, be lenient for her first night there,
The crib she slept in was so near my bed;
Her blue and white wool blanket was so soft;
Her pillow hollowed so to fit her head.

Teach me that she'll not want small rooms or me
When she has you and Heaven's immensity!

I always left a light out in the hall;
I hoped to make her fearless in the dark.
And yet – she was so small – one little light,
Not in the room, it scarcely mattered. Hark!

No, no! She seldom cried! God, not too far
For her to see, this first night, light a star!

And, in the morning, when she first woke up,
I always kissed her on the left cheek where
The dimple was. And, oh, I wet the brush!
It made it easier to curl her hair!

Just – just tomorrow morning, God, I pray,
When she wakes up, do things for her my way!

Violet Alleyn Storey

¶ This poem was at one time voted a favourite in the USA but it has proved impossible to trace any details about the author.

Tom John, *goldsmith and silversmith, grandson of Augustus John*

'In my trade all is won or lost in the soldering operation. We spend hours or days producing a part and it is when I start soldering these parts together that I call upon the Lord. My personal prayer usually is "Dear Lord… HELP". Then the relief when all is together and the solder has run in the right places is immense.'

Hugh Johnson, *author of books on wine and trees*

-+->-<-+-

Bénédicité

Que le bon Dieu nous bénisse, et toutes les bonnes choses qu'il
 aime bien nous donner.

'This was the favourite Grace before Meat of my old patron André Simon,
founder of the Wine & Food Society, champagne salesman and devout
Catholic (he lived in Carlyle Mansions so that he could go to Mass in
Westminster Cathedral every morning).'

Dr Lucy Johnson, *physician and geriatrician*

-+->-<-+-

Dear Lord,
I expect to pass through this world but once;
and any good thing, therefore, that I can do
or any kindness that I can show to any fellow creature,
let me do it now;
let me not defer or neglect it,
for I shall not pass this way again.

Stephen Grellet (1773–1855)

Martin Jolly, *Chairman of the National Hopgrowers' Conference*

→►◄←

Seventeenth-century Nun's Prayer

Lord, Thou knowest better than I know myself that I am growing older and will some day be old.

Keep me from the fatal habit of thinking I must say something on every subject and on every occasion. Release me from the craving to straighten out everybody's affairs. Make me thoughtful but not moody; helpful not bossy. With my vast store of wisdom it seems a pity not to use it all, but Thou knowest, Lord, that I want a few friends at the end.

Keep my mind free from the recital of endless details; give me wings to get to the point. Seal my lips on my aches and pains. They are increasing, and love of rehearsing them is becoming sweeter as years go by. I dare not ask for grace enough to enjoy the tales of others' pains, but help me to endure them with patience.

I dare not ask for improved memory, but for a growing humility and a lessening cocksureness when my memory seems to clash with the memories of others. Teach me the glorious lesson that occasionally I may be mistaken.

Keep me reasonably sweet; I do not want to be a saint – some of them are so hard to live with – but a sour old person is one of the crowning works of the devil. Give me the ability to see good things in unexpected places, and talents in unexpected people. And give me, Lord, the grace to tell them so.

Anon.

Virginia Jolly, *hopfarmer's wife and smallholder*

Un sourire ne coûte rien et apporte beaucoup. Il enrichit celui qui le reçoit sans appauvrir celui qui le donne.

Il ne dure qu'un instant mais son souvenir est parfois immortel.

Et pourtant il ne peut ni s'acheter, ni se prêter, ni se voler, car il n'a de valeur qu'à partir du moment où il se donne.

– et si on vous refuse le sourire que vous méritez, soyez généreux, donnez-lui le vôtre – pour l'amour de Dieu.

Source unknown

Look to this day, for it is life, the very life of life.
In its brief course lie all the realities and truths of existence.
The joy of growth, the splendour of action, the glory of power.
For yesterday is but a memory and tomorrow is only a vision.
But today well lived makes every yesterday a memory of happiness
and every tomorrow a vision of hope.
Look well, therefore, to this day!

Sanskrit poem

Deborah Jones, *Editor of the* Catholic Herald

St Basil's Prayer for Animals

O God, enlarge within us a sense of fellowship with all living things, our brothers and sisters the animals, to whom you gave the earth as their home in common with us.

We remember with shame that in the past we have exercised the high dominion of man with ruthless cruelty, so that the voice of the earth, which should have gone up to you in song, has been a groan of travail.

May we realize that they live not for us alone but for themselves and for you, and that they love the sweetness of life.

St Basil (330–79)

Keith, *life-sentenced prisoner*

-->-><-<-

Dear God,
I hold up all my weakness to your strength,
My failure to your faithfulness,
My sinfulness to your perfection,
My loneliness to your compassion,
My small pain to your agony on the cross. Amen.

¶ Keith wrote the prayer from which this is taken as an adaptation of one he found inscribed on the wall of his prison cell.

I cannot teach you how to pray in words. God listens not to your words save when He himself utters them through your lips. And I cannot teach you the prayer of the seas and the forests and the mountains. But you who are born of the mountains and the forests and the seas can find their prayer in your heart.

From *The Prophet* by Kahlil Gibran (1883–1931)

Tim Kirkbride, *retired company director*

-->-><-<-

From *A Cowboy's Prayer*

O Lord, I've never run where churches grow,
I've always loved Creation better as it stood
That day you finished it, so long ago,
And looked upon your work, and found it good.

Let me be easy on the man that's down
And make me square and generous with all;
I'm careless sometimes, Lord, when I'm in town,
But never let them call me mean or small.

'This prayer, in his own handwriting, was found among the books of the late Elliot Perkins, who trained as a cowboy in his youth, and later became Professor of History at Harvard University.'

Sir Robin Knox-Johnston, *master mariner*

✦

O Lord, if we are to die, I would rather it were in proceeding than in retreating.

'Attributed to John Davis (1550–1605), probably the greatest Elizabethan navigator.'

Stephen Lambert, *Master of Foxhounds*

✦

O Lord, give me patience, that throughout this day I may give the hounds room, and give myself time to greet others cheerfully along the way. Give me joy and optimism and an uncomplaining voice. Give me a thankful heart that I may ever be grateful for the wonders of Nature. These things I ask in the name of Jesus Christ, your Son.

Stephen Lambert

Lambeth Day Centre for the Homeless

✦

You continue to call us to work for peace.
Our world is broken and wounded by injustice, violence and
    indifference.
Alone, we would be overwhelmed by the challenges that face us.
But together, supported by your Spirit,
we can do more than any one of us could dream or imagine.

Written for the fiftieth anniversary of the Pax Christi International Movement in 1995

Admiral Sir Michael Layard

→>‹←

The Naval Prayer

O Eternal Lord God, who alone spreadest out the heavens, and rulest the raging of the sea; who hast compassed the waters with bounds until day and night come to an end; Be pleased to receive into thy Almighty and most gracious protection the persons of us thy servants and the Fleet in which we serve. Preserve us from the dangers of the sea, and of the air and the violence of the enemy; that we may be a safeguard unto our most gracious Sovereign Lady, Queen Elizabeth, and her Dominions, and a security for such as pass on the seas upon their lawful occasions; that the inhabitants of our Island may in peace and quietness serve thee our God; and that we may return in safety to enjoy the blessings of the land, with the fruits of our labours, and with a thankful remembrance of thy mercies to praise and glorify thy holy Name; through Jesus Christ our Lord. Amen.

Forms of prayer to be used at Sea, Book of Common Prayer

God bless all those that I love,
God bless all those that love me,
God bless all those that love those that I love
And all those that love those that love me.

Seventeenth-century New England sampler

John le Carré, *writer*

-+->-<-+-

Gentle Jesus, meek and mild,
Look upon a little child;
Pity my simplicity,
Suffer me to come to thee.

Charles Wesley (1707–88), from the *New English Hymnal*

Also chosen by:
John Gould, *cheddar cheese maker, Somerset; and* **Pamela Wooderson**, *housewife.*

'When I was very young, I prayed for mice, of which I was fond, and dorky birds, which I had never seen. It was a misunderstanding. I thought I was being told to 'pity mice implicitly'. The doorkeeper – but alas not the dorky bird – comes from Psalm 84, verse 10.'

Admiral of the Fleet Sir Henry Leach

-+->-<-+-

Lord, through this night may we be in Thy keeping,
Send Thou thy heavenly host to guard us sleeping.
O light of lights, be Thou our Light divine
And in our darkest hour – Lord keep us Thine.

From a hymn book formerly used at the Royal Naval College, Dartmouth

Hugh Leach, *retired diplomat*

-->-<-

Be strong. Be strong.
We are not here to dream,
To drift,
There are battles to fight,
And loads to lift;
Shun not the battle,
'Tis God's gift,
Be strong, be strong.
It matters not how
Deep entrenched the wrong,
How hard the fight, the day how long,
Faint not, fight on,
Tomorrow comes the song.
Be strong, be strong.

❡ Given to Hugh Leach by Lady Taylor, who had found it in her grandfather's Bible in 1935 and used it all her life.

Vouchsafe, O Lord, that I get through this day without being found out.

Unknown source

Caroline Lee, *countrywoman and garden centre helper*

-->-<-

Thank you, Lord, for the gift of our senses so that we may enjoy nature's gifts. From the first snowdrops of spring through summer's glory to autumn's harvest of fruits, we thank you, Lord. Help us, Lord, to draw strength from nature's continuing beauty so that we might be enriched and thereby able to enrich life for others.

Caroline Lee

Gary Lineker, *footballer*

-+>-<+-

Jerusalem

And did those feet in ancient time
    Walk upon England's mountains green?
And was the holy Lamb of God
    On England's pleasant pastures seen?
And did the Countenance Divine
    Shine forth upon our clouded hills?
And was Jerusalem builded here
    Among these dark Satanic Mills?

Bring me my Bow of burning gold!
    Bring me my Arrows of desire!
Bring me my Spear! O clouds, unfold!
    Bring me my Chariot of fire!
I will not cease from Mental Fight,
    Nor shall my Sword sleep in my hand,
Till we have built Jerusalem
    In England's green and pleasant land.

William Blake (1757–1827)

Also chosen by:
Julian Temperley, *cider brandy maker, Somerset.*

Ken Lingham, *Kent cereal and beef farmer*

-+>-<+-

Have mercy, O most gracious God, upon all men. Bless especially my father and mother, my brothers and sisters, my relatives and friends and all whom I love or who are kind to me. Bless also the clergy of this parish, have pity upon the sick and suffering. Give us food and clothing, keep us in good health, comfort us in all our troubles, make us to please Thee in all we do and bring us safe at last to our home in Heaven: Through Jesus Christ our Lord. Amen.

Charles Boyd

Bridget Litchfield, *Mother Prioress of the Carmelite Monastery, York*

→>-<←

What can I give him,
 Poor as I am?
If I were a shepherd
 I would bring a lamb;
If I were a wise man
 I would do my part;
Yet what I can I give him—
 Give my heart.

From 'In the bleak mid-winter' by Christina Rossetti (1830–94)

'This has been a favourite of mine since I was a child at Ashcott in Somerset.'

Julian Litchfield, *innkeeper, The Halfway House*

→>-<←

Give me good digestion, Lord,
And also something to digest.
Give me a healthy body, Lord,
With a sense to keep it at its best.
Give me a healthy mind, Good Lord,
To keep the pure and good in sight,
Which, seeing sin, is not appalled,
But finds a way to set it right.
Give me a mind that is not bored,
That does not whimper, whine or sigh.
Don't let me worry overmuch
About the fussy thing called 'I'.
Give me a sense of humour, Lord,
Give me the grace to see a joke,
To get some happiness in life,
And pass it on to other folk.

Sir Thomas More (1478–1535)

'This prayer is as applicable to a common innkeeper as it may have been to one of Sir Thomas's exalted position: I hope, however, that our eventual fates are greatly different!'

The Rt. Hon. the Earl of Longford

→>─<←

The sacrifices of God are a broken spirit: a broken and a contrite heart, O God, thou wilt not despise.

Psalm 51, verse 17 (Authorized Version)

'Visiting prisoners twice a week, I find this verse brings me close to everyone, whatever they may have done. It brings home to me more forcibly than anything else in the Bible, the kind of loving scrutiny to which we shall all be subjected in due course.'

Captain Jonathan Lyall, *RN, submariner*

→>─<←

He who eats and drinks, but does not bless the Lord, is a thief.

'This first grace I sometimes use when there seems to be a surfeit of food.'

Lord, grant that we may always be right,
For Thou knowest we are hard to turn.

'This second often seems appropriate for gatherings involving naval officers.'

Helen MacDonald-Hall,
gardener and whippet enthusiast

→>-<+-

If my soul has turned perversely to the dark;
If I have left some brother wounded by the way;
If I have preferred my aims to Thine;
If I have been impatient and would not wait;
If I have marred the pattern drawn out for my life;
If I have cost tears to those I loved;
If my heart has murmured against Thy will,
  O Lord, forgive.

F. B. Meyer

Pray for me as I will for thee that we may merrily meet in Heaven.

Sir Thomas More (1478–1535)

Gemma McKean, *pupil, Halesworth Middle School*

→>-<+-

O God, the stars above shine with all your glory
and the flowers below glow with colour.
But why all the fighting,
The wars, the anger?
I just want to paint your joy …
To paint the shade of green on each blade of grass,
or the silkiness of hair on the cat's back.
Please shine your light in my path. Amen.

Gemma McKean (aged 12)

Derek Mellor, *administrative director, Amitabha Buddhist Centre*

→>—<+—

May everyone be happy,
May everyone be free from misery,
May no one ever be separated from their happiness,
May everyone have equanimity, free from hatred and attachment.

Translated by Geshe Kelsang Gyatso Rinposhe from a traditional Tibetan source
derived from a Sanskrit original

The Rt. Hon. the Lord Menuhin, *violinist*

→>—<+—

To Thee Whom I do not and cannot know – within me and beyond me – I address this prayer:

Guide me to my better self – help me make myself into one who is trusted by most living things, keep me as one who respects the mystery and the character of every variety of life in both its uniqueness and its mass. Help me to be a good trustee for the body You gave me. No life is to do with as I will, not even my 'own', for it is an object of art, entrusted into 'my' temporary keeping.

May those who survive me not mourn but continue to be as helpful, kind and wise to others as they were to me. Although I would love to enjoy for many years the fruits of my lucky and rich life, with my family, music, friends, literature, many projects, and this whole world of diverse cultures and peoples – I have already received such blessings as would satisfy a thousand lives.

Help me in all confrontations to see the 'trialogue' as opposed to the 'dialogue'. Help me so that I may decide wisely on such apportionment of pleasure and pain as may fall within my jurisdiction.

Encourage me to revere and to follow those examples who enshrine your spirit – the spirit within and beyond each of us.

Thy will be done.

Excerpts taken from a prayer written by Lord Menuhin

Captain Richard Meryon, *RN*

＋＞＜＋

For this cause I bow my knees unto the Father of our Lord Jesus
    Christ,
That Christ may dwell in your hearts by faith; that ye, being rooted
    and grounded in love,
May be able to comprehend with all the saints what is the breadth,
    and length, and depth, and height;
And to know the love of Christ, which passeth knowledge, that ye
    might be filled with all the fulness of God.

Ephesians 3, verses 14 and 17–19 (Authorized Version)

David Moore, *cabinetmaker and teacher*

＋＞＜＋

I could see the lights in the windows of all the other houses on our
hill and hear the music rising from them up the long, steadily
falling night. I turned the gas down, I got into bed. I said some
words to the close and holy darkness, and then I slept.

From *A Child's Christmas in Wales* by Dylan Thomas (1914–53)

'I had much love for my mother-in-law and when she died recently, I
copied this and laid it, with other family tributes, on her grave.'

Bridget Moreton, *artist*

＋＞＜＋

Enlighten my soul that she may find her life and joy in Thee, until,
transported out of herself by the excess of her happiness, she binds
herself to Thee.

Dag Hammarskjöld (1905–61), translated by W. H. Auden

Charlotte Moreton, *ecologist*

→>—<←

Be sober, be vigilant; because your adversary the devil, as a roaring lion, walketh about, seeking whom he may devour: Whom resist steadfast in the faith.

1 Peter 5, verses 8–9 (Authorized Version)

¶ This passage is used in the Order of Compline.

Patrick Moreton, *student*

→>—<←

God indeed preserves the ship but the mariner conducts it into the harbour.

Erasmus (*c.*1467–1536)

David Morgan, *custodian, Glastonbury Abbey*

→>—<←

A Prayer for the Gurkha

O God, who in the Gurkha has given to mankind a race exceptional in courage and devotion and resplendent in cheerfulness. We, who owe the Gurkhas so much, ask your special blessing on them, their families and their land. Grant us your grace to be loyal to their best interest as they have been to ours in the past. Amen.

Attributed to J. R. Youens, a former Chaplain General

¶ Said at the Annual Reunion Memorial Service, Gurkha Brigade Association.

Philip Morlock, *retired fruit grower and shepherd*

→>–<←

Dear Lord, we thank You for all the wonderful gifts of this life; for the calm and serenity of a cool moonlit night, and the beauty of the fields, woods and countryside, and for our own senses and the ability to have, to see and to appreciate all these good gifts.

Above all we thank You for the gift of children, and for the joy they bring: may we never forget that they are Your children also, and that You have entrusted us with their care and nurturing so that they, in turn, may go forth to do Your will in their chosen paths of life.

Truly the best things in life are free and God-given.

May we, also, never forget those less fortunate than ourselves, that we may show compassion to them in their adversity. Amen.

Philip Morlock

Lady Morse, *London tourist guide*

→>–<←

[And] I said to the man who stood at the gate of the year: 'Give me a light that I may tread safely into the unknown.' And he replied: 'Go out into the darkness and put your hand into the hand of God. That shall be better than a light and safer than a known way.'

Minnie Louise Haskins, teacher and writer

'This prayer was quoted by King George VI in his Christmas Day broadcast, 25 December 1939. As a wartime child, I was given a postcard of it by my grandfather, which I read often (as children do). It had a reproduction of Holman Hunt's *Light of the World* illustrating it. I was interested, recently, to see it pinned up outside George VI's tomb/chapel at Windsor.'

Also chosen by:
David Ricketts, *accountant.*

Sir Jeremy Morse, *banker*

-+>-<+-

Blessed Lord, who hast caused all holy Scriptures to be written for our learning: Grant that we may in such wise hear them, read, mark, learn, and inwardly digest them, that by patience and comfort of thy holy Word, we may embrace, and ever hold fast the blessed hope of everlasting life, which thou hast given us in our Saviour Jesus Christ. Amen.

Collect for the second Sunday in Advent, Book of Common Prayer

The Rt. Hon. the Countess Mountbatten of Burma

-+>-<+-

Lord, grant that I may catch a fish
So large that even I,
In speaking of it afterwards,
May have no need to lie!

Source unknown

'This is a favourite of my husband, Lord Brabourne, who is a great fisherman.'

Also chosen by:
Robin Hanbury-Tenison, *traveller and writer.*

¶ Countess Mountbatten also chose the prayer attributed to St Francis, 'Make me an instrument of thy peace' (see page 53).

Olive Neumann, *housewife*

-+>-<+-

Teach me, my God and King,
In all things Thee to see;
And what I do in anything,
To do it as for Thee.

From 'The Elixir' by George Herbert (1593–1633)

Tim Newell, *prison governor*

→>⤛←

Keep me as the apple of an eye: hide me under the shadow of thy
 wings.

Psalm 17, verse 8 (Book of Common Prayer)

'I use this verse at times of difficulty or when things are going well. It has
been a source of strength for many years and puts me in the knowledge of
God's all-present love.'

Northern Ireland schoolchildren

→>⤛←

Peace in the city,
Peace in the house,
Peace in my heart,
And peace everywhere.

From 'A Prayer for Peace' by Joy Calvert, Londonderry Primary School,
and Alicia O'Rourke, St Finian's Primary

Please guide the leaders in our land to make this country a better
and safer place. Make all the war stop so that the people can live in
peace. Show us how to share what we have so that no one in the
world need be hungry.

From 'Peace' by Andrew McNeill, Londonderry Primary School,
and Ronan Dorrian, St Finian's Primary

¶ These prayers were written by schoolchildren of different denominations from
Newtownards, Northern Ireland, as part of a community relations programme.

Dear Lord God,
Even though we are different
Let us be grateful for the way you have made us and for the world
    we live in.
Let us talk people out of bombing and fighting.
Let us always respect others and try to think how they feel. Amen.

Sarah Eccles, Omagh Integrated School

❡ The integrated schools of Northern Ireland, which depend on voluntary support, bring the children of two cultures together in harmony.

Richard Ormond, *Director of the National Maritime Museum, Greenwich*

➤➤◄◄

A Vailima Prayer

Give us grace and strength
to forbear and to persevere.
Give us courage and gaiety
and the quiet mind.
Spare to us our friends, soften
to us our enemies. Bless us
if it may be in all our
innocent endeavours. If it
may not, give us the strength
to encounter that which is to
come, that we may be brave
in peril, constant in tribulation,
temperate in wrath.
And in all changes of fortune
And down to the gates of death
Loyal and loving
To one another.

Robert Louis Stevenson (1850–94)

❡ Stevenson died in Vailima on the island of Samoa, where he was known as Tusitala the Storyteller.

Shirley Orwell, *Somerset basket-maker*

→>—<←

Though your heart be sad within,
let cheer go out from you to others.
Meet them with a kindly presence,
considerate words and helpful acts.

'This prayer belonged to my father, and hung over his desk, framed, as it is now.'

Roger Overend, *Headmaster of the
Westminster Abbey Choir School*

→>—<←

The Gift of Silence

We are so busy, Lord, we do not listen.
The world is so noisy, Lord, we do not hear.
We do not hear what your spirit is saying to each one of us.
We have been afraid of silence.
Lord, teach us to use your gift of silence.
Teach us, Lord.

Written for Women's World Day of Prayer by women of New Zealand and included
in a collection made by Dorothy M. Stewart

The Rt. Hon. the Lord Owen, *politician and statesman*

+>-<+

The Physician's Prayer

From inability to let well alone, from too much zeal for the new and contempt for what is old, from putting knowledge before wisdom, science before art and cleverness before common sense, from treating patients as cases and from making the cure of the disease more grievous than the endurance of the same, good Lord deliver us.

Sir Robert Hutchison (1871–1960)

¶ Hutchison was Physician to the London Hospital and Great Ormond Street Hospital and President of the Royal College of Physicians. He was always keen to rid the medical profession of what he termed 'cant'.

Joe Parham, *solicitor's clerk*

Love

Love bade me welcome: yet my soul drew back,
        Guiltie of dust and sin.
But quick-ey'd Love, observing me grow slack
        From my first entrance in,
Drew nearer to me, sweetly questioning,
        If I lack'd anything.

A guest, I answer'd, worthy to be here:
        Love said, you shall be he.
I the unkinde, ungrateful? Ah my deare,
        I cannot look on thee.
Love took my hand and smiling did reply:
        Who made the eyes but I?

Truth, Lord, but I have marr'd them: let my shame
        Go where it doth deserve.
And know you not, sayes Love, who bore the blame?
        My deare, then I will serve.
You must sit down, sayes Love, and taste my meat:
        So I did sit and eat.

George Herbert (1593–1633)

Paul Partridge, *scrap metal merchant*

For thee, my God, the living God,
My thirsty soul doth pine;
O when shall I behold thy face,
Thou majesty divine?

From 'As pants the hart for cooling streams' by N. Tate (1652–1715) and N. Brady
(1659–1726), from Psalm 42

The Rt. Hon. Christopher Patten,
last Governor of Hong Kong

A Meditation

GOD has created me to do Him some definite service; He has committed some work to me which He has not committed to another. I have my mission – I may never know it in this life, but I shall be told it in the next.

I am a link in a chain, a bond of connection between persons. He has not created me for naught. I shall do good, I shall do His work. I shall be an angel of peace, a preacher of truth in my own place while not intending it – if I do but keep His Commandments.

Therefore, I will trust Him. Whatever, wherever I am, I can never be thrown away. If I am in sickness, my sickness may serve Him; in perplexity, my perplexity may serve Him; if I am in sorrow, my sorrow may serve Him. He does nothing in vain. He knows what He is about. He may take away my friends, He may throw me among strangers, He may make me feel desolate, make my spirits sink, hide my future from me – still He knows what He is about.

John Henry Newman (1801–90)

The Very Revd John F. Petty, *Provost of Coventry*

→>‹‹←

Death of a Child

Eternal God, from whom every family in heaven and earth
    takes its name,
we remember today our child whom you lent us to love and is
    now taken from us.
Hold each one in peace today and forever,
and as we offer you our memories of their unfinished lives,
bring us at last to rejoice together in that light and love that
    have no end;
through your own Child who died and was raised to glory,
our Saviour Jesus Christ. Amen.

Michael Sadgrove, Provost of Sheffield

A Coventry Prayer

Almighty God, Father of us all,
you call us to make peace and to love and serve our neighbour.
May our City (and Cathedral) ruined and rebuilt,
be a sign to all peoples of the healing of old wounds.
Help us to build a kinder, more just world
where those of many races may live together in peace,
and all the human family be one;
through Jesus Christ our Lord. Amen.

Michael Sadgrove, Provost of Sheffield

Richard Pitman, *broadcaster and former National Hunt jockey*

--><--

The Prayer of a Grand National Jockey

Lord, I can't see a thing in this mad gallop to the first fence.
Open a gap between horses or at least keep the leaders on their feet.
Beecher's Brook approaches, the landing drop awaits, it's a trap!
Stop my horse from over-balancing, keep his tail behind his ears.
The Canal turn is a right angle, guide us across while the rest go on
    straight.
Save us lengths in the air here, it could eventually win us the race.
The fifteenth is the Chair, the widest and highest of all,
Give courage to the loose horses, don't let them wipe me out now.
The Water is next, it's easy I know. The crowd is cheering with
another circuit to go. They want us to win, we're their favourite you
    see.
We've played survivors so far, now it's tactics we need,
ride with me, God, and to hell with the rest.
A crash at the next and the world turns upside down, the others
    jump
over us, we matter no more. Oh why desert me, did we not have a
    deal?
As they gallop away to glory for one, mine's only mental and
    physical pain. But it's clear at last, Lord, I've done it again.
I demanded your help without any acknowledgement of your right
to decide. I'm not worthy for help from you or your son.
It's a year to the day since I last asked the same favours and in that
    twelve months I never gave you a thought.
It is justice today and a lesson well taught.

Richard Pitman

Ken Poole, *newspaper deliverer*

→>—<←

Dear Lord, once again we ask your help with this our prayer for peace. Grant us to seek the ways of talking and meeting instead of the ways of guns and war and that whatever our colour or creed we may be as one.

Ken Poole

John Powderly, *consultant and facilitator*

→>—<←

The Hermit

I am the Hermit that guides you to the land of higher self. I am the Star the wise men followed. I can lead you on to new birth, the realization of all that is, all that you can be, and will become.

When in fear or unhappiness, seek my hand, I will be there. I am the part of you that sees the *way* clearly through the mists that cloud the mind. Trust me, and in the stillness of your mind I will guide you.

You must see that I guide you not just towards spirit, but also into matter. With one hand I hold the lamp that illuminates the thread of destiny, with the other I hold out the staff that you may follow my guide. I am the Helmsman, you the ship.

Consider the situations you find yourself in – they are all opportunities for growth; use them well.

In life you must grow and change. Consider the forest, it is constantly growing, never does it try to stay the same, neither does it wish to be the mountain or the sea, for it knows that it is perfectly placed being what it truly is.

You must nurture love and understanding, embrace joy and sorrow, live for the good times and the bad times for in reality they are the same. Live life to the full and give what you will.

Stephen Pope, biblical scholar and theologian

Robert Powell, *actor*

Da mihi castitatem et continentiam, sed noli modo.
(Give me chastity and continence, but not yet.)

St Augustine (354–430)

Elizabeth Raeburn, *potter*

If on a Spring night I went by
And God were standing there,
What is the prayer that I would cry
To Him? This is the prayer:

O Lord of courage grave,
O Master of this night of Spring!
Make firm in me a heart too brave
To ask Thee anything!

John Galsworthy (1867–1933)

The Revd Dr Konrad Raiser, *General Secretary of the World Council of Churches*

Lead us from death to life,
from falsehood to truth.
Lead us from despair to hope,
from fear to trust.
Lead us from hate to love,
from war to peace.
Let peace fill our heart, our world, our universe.

Anglican Church of Aotearoa/New Zealand and Polynesia

⁋ Used in the Worship Book of the World Council of Churches, 1983.

The Revd Dr Susan Ramsaran, *parish priest*

→>-<-

O Lord, may the end of my life be the best of it;
may my closing acts be my best acts;
and may the best of my days be the day when I shall meet Thee.

Unknown source

Also chosen by:
The Revd Canon Michael Cooper, *Hon. Canon Emeritus, Canterbury Cathedral.*

Sir David Ramsbotham, *HM Chief Inspector of Prisons*

→>-<-

Dear God,
Help me to take the right path in life and
Help me to know right from wrong.
Show me a way to get through life and its problems
No matter how hard they are.
Help me to build a life I can be proud of and
Show me the way to make a happy life.
I put my trust in You as You are a God Who loves
Us all no matter who we are.

Craig Adams (written when he was a young offender)

Marjorie Reeves, *historian, university teacher and retired Vice-Principal, St Anne's College, Oxford*

→>-<-

Bless us, O God, with the vision of Thy Being and beauty, that in the joy of Thy strength we may work without haste and without sloth, through Jesus Christ our Lord.

'This prayer, which I have used many times since my student days in SCM, is taken from J. H. Oldham, *A Devotional Diary* (1925), but its original source is unknown.'

John Reid, *flat-race jockey*

Derby Day

Dear Lord, on this day, a special day in racing terms,
I pray to you to guide us all.
The stakes are high, the pressure immense;
I feel the tension mount.
The normal smiling faces have a sterner look today.
The big day takes its toll,
The winning chance,
The chance of fame,
The chance to please.
Lord, help us all to keep our heads,
To come back safe both horse and man,
To hear the cheers whoever wins. Amen.

John Reid

David Rice, *stonemason and volunteer fireman*

The Church's one foundation is Jesus Christ her Lord;
She is his new creation by water and the word:
From heaven he came and sought her to be his holy Bride;
With his own Blood he bought her, and for her life he died.

Samuel J. Stone (1839–1900)

¶ David Rice worked for 50 years on the fabric of Wells Cathedral, particularly the
West front, on which stands the glory of Wells, the largest collection of medieval
statues in the British Isles.

Sir Cliff Richard, *singer*

When I survey the wondrous cross
On which the Prince of Glory died,
My richest gain I count but loss,
And pour contempt on all my pride.

Were the whole realm of nature mine,
That were an offering far too small;
Love so amazing, so divine,
Demands my soul, my life, my all.

Isaac Watts (1674–1748)

Dr Michael Richards, *general practitioner*

I have told you these things so that in me you may have perfect peace and confidence. In the world you have tribulation and trials and distress and frustration; but be of good cheer, take courage, be confident, certain, undaunted, for I have overcome the world. I have deprived it of power to harm, have conquered it for you.

John 16, verse 33 (Amplified Bible)

'There are times when prayers and readings seem to me to say exactly the right things.'

Dame Diana Rigg, *actress*

God bless Mama and Papa,
Willy and Ludo
And all the people I love.
God bless those who have no love,
Those who are ill and those who are hungry.
Please, God, bring them comfort. Amen.

'This is the prayer that I wrote for my daughter to say at night when she was very small.'

The Revd Prebendary Patrick Riley, *Vicar of the Abbey Five, Glastonbury*

-->--<--

The Glastonbury Prayer

God bless Glastonbury,
Inspire our leaders,
Guide our people,
Guard the elderly,
Protect the children,
Heal the sick,
Renew our churches.
Through Jesus Christ our Lord.

Rosemary Turnbull

Andrew Roberts, *historian*

-->--<--

In the ever-evolving world which You created, help us to tell the difference between change for Your sake and change for change's sake.

Andrew Roberts

Lord Rothermere, *newspaper proprietor*

-->--<--

If you can keep your head when all about you
Are losing theirs and blaming it on you,
If you can trust yourself when all men doubt you,
But make allowance for their doubting too;
If you can wait and not be tired by waiting,
Or being lied about, don't deal in lies,
Or being hated, don't give way to hating,
And yet don't look too good, nor talk too wise:

If you can fill the unforgiving minute
With sixty seconds' worth of distance run,
Yours is the Earth and everything that's in it,
And – which is more – you'll be a Man, my son!

From 'If——' by Rudyard Kipling (1865–1936)

The Rt. Revd the Rt. Hon. Lord Runcie

→>-<-

Saint Teresa's Bookmark

Let nothing disturb thee,
Nothing affright thee;
All things are passing:
God never changeth:
Patient endurance
Attaineth to all things:
Who God possesseth
In nothing is wanting.
Alone God sufficeth.

St Teresa of Avila (1515–82)

'This is a little prayer or meditation which I have printed at the beginning of my Prayer Book. I keep it in mind all the time. So it is something which has steadied me and strengthened me in times of trial and moments of doubt. In a long life I have had plenty of these.'

Also chosen by:
Bridget Litchfield, *Mother Prioress, Carmelite Monastery, York.*

¶ Lord Runcie also sent a prayer which is pinned above the desk of a holy nun, a friend of his. It simply says,

God bless this mess.

Ashlea Russell, *pupil*

✦

God Made Spring

God made daffodils like golden dancers,
Primroses yellow and bright,
Snowdrops like little prancers,
Bluebells blue or white.
Bugs with backs like shields,
Foals galloping across fields,
Blackbirds and skylarks that love to sing,
Remember that God made Spring.

Ashlea Russell, aged 10

Dr Jonathan Sacks, *Chief Rabbi*

✦

O my God, the soul which You placed within me is pure.
You created it, You formed it, You breathed it into me, and You
preserve it within me.
You will one day take it from me, but will restore it to me in the
hereafter.
So long as the soul is within me, I will give thanks to You, O Lord
my God and God of my fathers, Master of all works, Lord of all
souls. Blessed are You – the Lord, who restores the souls to the
dead.

Ancient Jewish Traditional

'This prayer, taken from the daily morning service of the Jewish prayer
book, affirms the essential goodness of humanity, the gift of life itself, and
our need to be mindful that it is given to us by G–d in order to do good
while we are here on earth.'

Tessa Sanderson, *athlete*

→>-<←

If, through the unguarded moment of the evening,
sadness has crept into your heart,
Let it sail away with the setting sun
Because tonight is God's night for peacemaking.

'There have been so many times in my life that I have called unto the Lord our Heavenly Father, not just for myself but also for the hope of others. With this in mind I recall a special moment in which a friend wrote this verse of hope for me. I have never forgotten it.'

The Rt. Revd Mark Santer, *Bishop of Birmingham*

→>-<←

We adore you, Lord Jesus Christ, here and in all your churches throughout the world, and we bless you, because by your holy cross you have redeemed the world.

St Francis of Assisi

'This prayer is for use when someone goes into a church. It can be reliably attributed to St Francis of Assisi, unlike the more popular and beautiful "Make me an instrument of your peace", which first appeared in the 1920s.'

Richard Sargent, *school bursar*

→>-<←

O Lord of the sunshine and the starlight, who hast set us in a green land of vale and hill and meadow, we thank thee for the springtime with its flowers and fresh grass, we praise thee for the long afternoons of summer, when the shadows lengthen across the cricket field, we bless thee for the glories of autumn, with its falling leaves and mellow fruits.

Grant us to see the lessons of the lilies, and when the city with its streets hides us from the world of nature, may the skies above the roofs remind us of thine eternal beauty ever present. In days of dullness help us to carry the beauty of the daffodils in our minds, and the song of the birds in our hearts: for Christ's sake. Amen.

'This prayer by J. B. Goodliffe was used at my preparatory school.'

Dame Cicely Saunders, *Chairman of St Christopher's Hospice, founder of the hospice movement*

+>-<+

My lord god, I have no idea where I am going. I do not see the road ahead of me. I cannot know for certain where it will end. Nor do I really know myself, and the fact that I think that I am following your will does not mean that I am actually doing so. But I believe that the desire to please you does in fact please you. And I hope I have that desire in all that I am doing. I hope that I will never do anything apart from that desire. And I know that if I do this you will lead me by the right road though I may know nothing about it. Therefore I will trust you always though I may seem to be lost and in the shadow of death. I will not fear, for you are ever with me, and you will never leave me to face my perils alone.

Thomas Merton (1915–68), a mystic and a Trappist monk of the Abbey of Gethsemani, Kentucky

'I carry this prayer about with me all the time in my diary and have used it often in hospice meetings.'

¶ Dame Cicely found this prayer in Gethsemani monastery on a visit many years ago.

Josephine Sawney, *organist*

Of what avail this restless, hurrying activity?
This heavy weight of earthly duties?
God's purposes stand firm,
And thou, His little one,
Needest one thing alone,
Trust in His power and He will meet thy need,
Thy burden resteth safe on Him;
And thou, His little one,
Mayest play securely at His side.
This is the sum and substance of it all.
God is,
God loveth thee,
God beareth all thy care.

Tukaram (1608–49), Indian peasant and mystic

Chosen in gratitude to Sanjli Raja, 'who taught me in her life the truth of this prayer'.

The Rt. Hon. Lord Justice Schiemann, *Lord Justice of Appeal*

→>-<+-

The Study of Law

Almighty God, Giver of Wisdom, without Whose help resolutions are vain, without Whose blessing study is ineffectual, enable me, if it be Thy will, to attain such knowledge as may qualify me to direct the doubtful, and instruct the ignorant, to prevent wrongs, and terminate contentions; and grant that I may use that knowledge, which I shall attain, to Thy glory and my own salvation, for Jesus Christ's sake.

Doctor Samuel Johnson (1709–84)

O Lord, my Maker and Protector, Who has graciously sent me into this world, to work out my salvation, enable me to drive from me all such unquiet and perplexing thoughts as may mislead or hinder me in the practice of those duties which Thou hast required. When I behold the works of Thy hands and consider the course of Thy providence, give me Grace always to remember that Thy thoughts are not my thoughts, nor Thy ways my ways. And while it shall please Thee to continue me in this world where much is to be done and little is to be known, teach me by Thy Holy Spirit to withdraw my mind from unprofitable and dangerous enquiries, from difficulties vainly curious, and doubts impossible to be solved. Let me rejoice in the light which Thou hast imparted, let me serve Thee with active zeal, and humble confidence, and wait with patient expectation for the time in which the soul which Thou receivest, shall be satisfied with knowledge. Grant this, O Lord, for Jesus Christ's sake.

Doctor Samuel Johnson (1709–84)

'I first came across this second prayer at Cambridge, and have found it a useful corrective when I discover myself engaged in pursuing "difficulties vainly curious, and doubts impossible to be solved"; I rather enjoy the elegance of eighteenth-century writing.'

Mary Schlich, *retired teacher*

✦✦✦

Help us to live out what we know in
our hearts to be true,
that all things come from you
and it is only your own that
we give you.

Draw us beyond the bounds of
the Church to work your will
and offer your love to those who
secretly long for it,
for in doing your will we also
receive your love.

From a prayer written by Mary Schlich for Christian Stewardship, 1997

David Schreiber, *management consultant*

✦✦✦

A Sufi Prayer

Do to me what is worthy of Thee
And not what is worthy of me.

From *The Gulistan* (Rose Garden) by Saadi of Shiraz, Persian classical author of the
thirteenth century

Lady Scott

✦✦✦

Silently, one by one, in the infinite meadows of heaven, blossomed
the lovely stars, the forget-me-nots of the angels.

Henry Wadsworth Longfellow (1807–82)

Sir Harry Secombe, *singer and entertainer*

✦

O Lord, support us all the day long of this troublous life, until the shades lengthen and the evening comes, the busy world is hushed, the fever of life is over, and our work done.

Then, Lord, in Thy mercy, grant us safe lodging, a holy rest, and peace at the last, through Jesus Christ, our Lord. Amen.

John Henry Newman (1801–90)

Also chosen by:
Eileen Lees, *former national chairman of the Cookery and Food Association;*
Lord Montagu of Beaulieu *(this prayer is in his family graveyard at Beaulieu);*
and **Roger Stacey**, *choral society conductor, Somerset.*

The Revd Norman Shanks, *Leader of the Iona Community*

✦

O Christ, you are within each of us. It is not just the interior of these walls; it is our own inner being you have renewed. We are your temple not made with hands. We are your body. If every wall should crumble, and every church decay, we are your habitation. Nearer are you than breathing, closer than hands and feet. Ours are the eyes with which you, in the mystery, look out in compassion on the world. Yet we bless you for this place, for your directing of us, your redeeming of us, and your indwelling. Take us outside, Lord, outside holiness, out to where soldiers curse and nations clash at the crossroads of the world. So shall this building continue to be justified. We ask it for your own name's sake. Amen.

George MacLeod, founder of the Iona Community

'This prayer is used every Thursday morning in Iona Abbey.'

Om Parkash Sharma, *President of the National Council of Hindu Temples (UK)*

➤➤◄◄

May the world be peaceful. May the wicked become gentle. May all creatures think of mutual welfare. May their minds be occupied with what is auspicious. And may our hearts be immersed in selfless love for the Lord.

From the *Shremad Bhagwat Puran* (V.18.9)

Dame Barbara Shenfield, *former Chairman of the WRVS*

➤➤◄◄

O Lord,
'How small, of all that human hearts endure,
That part which laws or kings can cause or cure!'
I put my trust in Thee.

From *The Traveller* by Oliver Goldsmith (1728–74)

Giles Shepard, *manager of the Ritz Hotel*

➤➤◄◄

Sis bonus puer, docilis et verecundus, ita caste integreque adolescens inter aequales tuos, ut tandem ex scholari disciplina evadas civis honestus ac patriae utilis, ad maiorem Dei gloriam, per Jesum Christum Dominum nostrum.

(Be a good boy, obedient and modest, a young man so pure and true amongst your contemporaries that, as a result of your training at school, you emerge an honourable citizen, useful to your country, to the greater glory of God, through Jesus Christ Our Lord.)

'This prayer comes from Eton and was read to scholars on arrival by the Provost.'

The Rt. Revd David Sheppard, *Bishop of Liverpool*

➤➤◄◄

Almighty God,
You have provided the resources of the world
To maintain the life of your children,
And have so ordered our life
That we are dependent upon each other.

Bless all people in their daily work,
And, as you have given us the knowledge to produce plenty,
So give us the will to bring it within reach of all;
Through Jesus Christ Our Lord. Amen.

Collect for Rogation Days, Alternative Service Book 1980

Judy Shercliff, *teacher and volunteer cathedral guide*

➤➤◄◄

If I should go before the rest of you
Break not a flower nor inscribe a stone,
Nor when I'm gone speak in a Sunday voice
But be the usual selves that I have known.
  Weep if you must,
  Parting is hell,
  But life goes on,
  So sing as well.

Joyce Grenfell (1910–79)

Mark Shercliff, *pupil, Wells Cathedral School*

➤►◄◄

From *'Arglwydd arwain trwy'r anialwch'*

Guide me, O thou great Jehovah,
Pilgrim through this barren land;
I am weak but thou art mighty;
Hold me with thy powerful hand.

William Williams (1716–91), translated by Peter Williams (1727–96) and others

'This hymn used to be sung by Welsh miners at the end of a shift. For me, it evokes Sunday evensong in the Cathedral as well as the singing in a packed stadium.'

Dennis Silk, *retired headmaster,* *and former President of MCC and the TCCB*

➤►◄◄

Lord, be patient with us, and help us to be patient with you, that in the fullness of time we may understand better our need for you. When that understanding dawns, bring us into your kingdom as willing servants and faithful friends. We ask this for your name's sake.

❡ Written by Dennis Silk while a housemaster at Marlborough and used for evening prayers.

Nikki Slade, *trumpeter and actress*

→>-<-

Dear Jesus, help me to spread Your fragrance everywhere I go.
Flood my soul with Your spirit and life.
Penetrate and possess my whole being, so utterly,
That my life may only be a radiance of Yours.
Shine through me, and be so in me,
That every soul I come in contact with
        may feel Your presence in my soul.
Let them look up and see no longer me,
        but only Jesus!
Stay with me, and then I shall begin to
        shine as You shine;
So to shine as to be a light to others.

John Henry Newman (1801–90)

❡ Mother Teresa (1910–97), of the Missionaries of Charity, Calcutta, recounted that this prayer is recited by the sisters daily.

Delia Smith, *cook and author*

→>-<-

Come, Holy Spirit, fill the hearts of your faithful.
And kindle in them the fire of your love.

Send forth your Spirit and they shall be created.
And you shall renew the face of the earth.

❡ An invocation to the Holy Spirit partly derived from Psalm 104. Traditionally used on Whit Sunday, it is now in more general use.

Lois Smith, *pupil, Halesworth Middle School, Suffolk*

-+>-<+-

The Prayer of the Turtle

O God, let me be free of this weighty shell upon my back.
When I'm swimming freely in the cool dark water
it is a great discomfort to be weighed down
by this, this piece of bone.
But if I didn't have a shell …
I wouldn't be a turtle! Amen.

Lois Smith (aged 13 years)

Rosemary Smyth, *miller's wife*

-+>-<+-

From the prison of anxious thought that greed has builded,
From the fetters that envy has wrought, and pride has gilded,
From the noise of the crowded ways and the fierce confusion,
From the folly that wastes its days in a world of illusion,
(Ah, but the life is lost that frets and languishes there!)
I would escape and be free in the joy of the open air.

By the faith that the flowers show when they bloom unbidden,
By the calm of the river's flow to a goal that is hidden,
By the trust of the tree that clings to its deep foundation,
By the courage of wild birds' wings on the long migration,
(Wonderful secret of peace that abides in Nature's breast!)
Teach me how to confide, and live my life, and rest.

H. van Dyke (1852–1933)

¶ A prolific writer on nature, in 1917 Van Dyke resigned his post as a Presbyterian minister in the Netherlands, being unable to reconcile living in a neutral country with his desire to raise opinion against the German threat.

The troubles of my heart are enlarged: O bring thou me out of my
   distresses.

Psalm 25, verse 17 (Authorized Version)

'A prayer for a difficult time.'

The Rt. Revd David Stancliffe, *Bishop of Salisbury*

Blessed are you, Lord our God, lover of souls:
you uphold us in life and sustain us in death:
to you be glory and praise for ever!
For the darkness of this age is passing away
as Christ the bright and morning star
brings to his saints the light of life.
As you give light to those in darkness
who walk in the shadow of death,
so remember in your kingdom your faithful servants,
that death may be for them the gate to life
and to unending fellowship with you;
where with your saints you live and reign,
one in the perfect union of love
now and for ever. Amen.

❡ Written by Bishop Stancliffe for use at All Souls or any commemoration of the dead.

Sarah Stancliffe, *bishop's wife*

→>·<←

We are no longer on our own, but yours.
Put us to what you will, rank us with whom you will;
put us to doing, put us to suffering;
let us be employed for you or laid aside for you,
exalted for you or brought low for you;
let us be full, let us be empty;
let us have all things, let us have nothing.
We freely and wholeheartedly yield all things to your
pleasure and disposal.

And now, glorious and blessed God,
Father, Son, and Holy Spirit,
you are ours and we are yours.
So be it.
And the covenant which we made on earth,
let it be ratified in heaven.

From the Methodist Covenant Prayer

'This is a prayer for those in public life or embarking on retirement, a good antidote for those of us who revel in busyness; I find it helpful in this strange life where one moment I am in the relative limelight, the next, shifting chairs or seeming unneeded.'

The Royalist Grace (before meals)

Lord, send this Crumb well down.

Lindsay Staniforth, *teacher and writer*

→>⤚

Sanjaya addresses Krishna

Thou God from the beginning, God in man since man was. Thou Treasure supreme of this vast universe. Thou the One to be known and the Knower, the final resting place. Thou infinite Presence in whom all things are.

God of the winds and the waters, of fire and death! Lord of the solitary moon, the Creator, the Ancestor of all! Adoration unto thee, a thousand adorations; and again and again unto thee adoration.

Adoration unto thee who art before me and behind me: adoration unto thee who art on all sides, God of all. All powerful God of immeasurable might. Thou art the consummation of all: thou art all.

Bhagavad Gita, II, verses 38, 39, 40

Lord of Creation, may my every guest
By all my kitchen skill be much impressed.
I know you were content with loaves and fishes,
But these days they expect less homely dishes.
May they not spot the traps I've set for mice,
But be beguiled by scents of bread and spice;
Let meals run smoothly from the rough terrine
To summer pudding with sauce mousseline.
And please, Lord, let them never ever guess
It's mostly been acquired at M and S.

Lindsay Staniforth

Lady Staveley

✦

Thou wilt keep him in perfect peace, whose mind is stayed on thee: . . .

From Isaiah 26, verse 3 (Authorized Version)

O God, forasmuch as without thee we are not able to please thee; Mercifully grant that thy Holy Spirit may in all things direct and rule our hearts; through Jesus Christ our Lord. Amen.

Collect for the nineteenth Sunday after Trinity, Book of Common Prayer

'Universally used, I have known this prayer by heart for very many years.'

Ann Steadman, *retired headteacher of a primary school in Edinburgh*

✦

It were as easy for Jesu
To renew the withered tree
As to wither the new
Were it His will so to do.
     Jesu! Jesu! Jesu!
     Jesu! meet it were to praise Him.

There is no plant in the ground
But is full of His virtue,
There is no form in the strand
But is full of His blessing
     Jesu! Jesu! Jesu!
     Jesu! meet it were to praise Him.

There is no life in the sea,
There is no creature in the river,
There is naught in the firmament,
But proclaims His goodness.
     Jesu! Jesu! Jesu!
     Jesu! meet it were to praise Him.

There is no bird on the wing,
There is no star in the sky,
There is nothing beneath the sun,
But proclaims His goodness.
Jesu! Jesu! Jesu!
Jesu! meet it were to praise Him.

From *Carmina Gadelica,* collected and translated by Alexander Carmichael
(1832–1912)

A medieval invocation from the Hebrides. The author, a leper, was apparently miraculously cured on the Isle of Harris, where she was obliged to live alone on the seashore. It is possible that her diet of shellfish and shore plants aided the cure. A similar diet may have been given to leper pilgrims at the shrine of St James of Compostela in Spain.

Ronald Stevenson, *composer*

→>–<←

The day returns and brings us the petty round of irritating concerns and duties. Help us to play the man, help us to perform them with laughter and kind faces, let cheerfulness abound with industry. Give us to go blithely on our business all this day, bring us to our resting beds weary and content and undishonoured, and grant us in the end the gift of sleep.

Robert Louis Stevenson (1850–94)

'I choose a prayer by my namesake, (Robert Louis) Stevenson. As a schoolboy I attended daily morning service with hymns. One of the prayers was the one I have chosen. What I particularly appreciate about RLS's Vailima Prayers, written in the South Seas for family use, is their brightness and gaiety.'

Rosamund Strode, *formerly music assistant to Sir Benjamin Britten*

✦✦✦

Antiphon

Chorus: Praised be the God of love,
      Men: Here below,
      Angels: And here above:
Chorus: Who hath dealt his mercies so,
      Angels: To his friend,
      Men: And to his foe;

Chorus: That both grace and glorie tend
      Angels: Us of old,
      Men: And us in th'end.
Chorus: The great shepherd of the fold
      Angels: Us did make,
      Men: For us was sold.

Chorus: He our foes in pieces brake;
      Angels: Him we touch;
      Men: And him we take.

Chorus: Wherefore since that he is such,
      Angels: We adore,
      Men: And we do crouch.

Chorus: Lord, Thy praises should be more.
      Men: We have none,
      Angels: And we no store,

Chorus: Praised be the God alone,
      Who hath made of two folds one.

George Herbert (1593–1633)

'The beauty of the setting suggest that these words struck a particular chord for Britten. The end of the chorus becomes a harmonic struggle between angels and men who pursue remote harmonies before uniting with the angels in the ultimate, harmonic "one".'

Pat Stuart, *diplomat's wife and housewife*

→>⋅<⋅

We seem to give them back to You, O God, who gave them to us. Yet as You did not lose them in giving, so we do not lose them by their return. Not as the world gives, do You give, O lover of souls. What You give, take not away, for what is Yours is ours also if we are Yours. And life is eternal and love is immortal, and death is only a horizon, and a horizon is nothing save the limit of our sight. Lift us up, strong Son of God, that we may see further; cleanse our eyes that we may see more clearly; draw us closer to Yourself that we may know ourselves to be nearer to our loved ones who are with You. And while You prepare a place for us, prepare us also for that happy place that where You are we may be also for evermore.

Bishop Brent (1862–1926)

Philip Sturrock, *publisher*

→>⋅<⋅

Christ in Woolworth's

I did not think to find you there –
Crucifixes, large and small,
Sixpence and threepence, on a tray,
Among the artificial pearls,
Paste rings, tin watches, beads of glass.
It seemed so strange to find you there
Fingered by people coarse and crass,
Who had no reverence at all.
Yet – what is it you would say?
'For these I hang upon my cross,
For these the agony and loss,
Though heedlessly they pass Me by.'
Dear Lord forgive such fools as I
Who thought it strange to find you there
When you are with us everywhere.

Teresa Hooley

Bez Swinton-Berry, *engraver*

—➤—◄—

To see a World in a Grain of Sand,
    And a Heaven in a Wild Flower,
Hold Infinity in the palm of your hand,
    And Eternity in an hour.

From *Auguries of Innocence* by William Blake (1757–1827)

'I admire Blake as a philosopher, mystic and fellow engraver. Unwittingly I settled in Lambeth, close to his home in Hercules Road.'

The Revd Dr John B. Taylor, *President of the Methodist Conference (1997–98)*

—➤—◄—

O Christ the Light,
illuminate and cleanse the dark corners of the world
where hang the cobwebs of apathy
and the dust of neglect;
shine on faces made grim
by poverty and war;
melt the icicles of despair
and the hard frozen wastes
of selfishness;
and let your searching rays
enclose the whole
in one great radiance.

'I find this prayer, written by a Methodist, Betty Hares, for many years a Mission Partner in West Africa, very moving.'

Mary Taylor, *patient in St Thomas's Hospital*

→>—<—

Gracious and Holy Father,
Give us wisdom to perceive You,
intelligence to understand You,
diligence to seek You,
patience to wait for You,
eyes to behold You,
hearts to meditate upon You,
and life to proclaim You,
through the power of the Holy Spirit of Jesus Christ, our Lord.

St Benedict (*c*.480–*c*.547)

Also chosen by:
Leonard Taylor, *lay preacher, United Reform Church.*

Dame Kiri Te Kanawa, *opera singer*

→>-<←

Desdemona's Prayer before Her Death

(She goes to the prie-dieu.)

Prega per chi adorando a te si prostra,
Prega pel peccator, per l'innocente,
E pel debole oppresso e pel possente,
Misero anch'esso, tua pièta dimostra.
Prega per chi sotto l'oltraggio piega
La fronte e sotto la malvagia sorte;
Per noi tu prega
Sempre e nell'ora della nostra morte.

(She remains kneeling at the prie-dieu as if in silent prayer.
Only the first and last words of the prayer can be heard.)

Ave Maria...............
...........nell'ora della morte.
Amen.

(Pray for those who humbly kneel before thee,
Pray for those who sin, and for the sinless,
Pray for all who know oppression, and for the oppressor,
He too is wretched, and he needs thy pardon.
Pray for a maiden whose heart must bear
Cruel grief, who suffers from unjust suspicion;
As we implore thee, pray for us
Ever while we are living, in the hour of dying.
Ave Maria ....
...........in the hour of dying.
Amen.)

From Act IV, scene 2, of *Otello* by Giuseppe Verdi (1813–1901),
libretto by Arrigo Boito (1842–1918); translated by Andrew Porter

¶ A quarrel between Verdi and Boito had been resolved by Verdi's publisher. The poet wrote an inspired libretto which stimulated Verdi, aged 74, to compose what many consider to be his crowning masterpiece.

The Rt. Hon. Baroness Thatcher

Thou, O Lord, that stillest the raging of the sea, hear, hear us, and
save us, that we perish not.

From 'Short Prayers in respect of a Storm', Forms of Prayer to be used at Sea, Book of
Common Prayer

'This prayer would seem equally appropriate to politics.'

❡ Baroness Thatcher also chose a beautiful prayer on the theme of being true to one's
self and to the vows made in one's youth. Sadly, it was not possible to obtain copyright for the prayer.

Jennie Thomas, *art teacher*

May the glory of the LORD endure for ever;
   may the LORD rejoice in his works.

He looks at the earth, and it trembles;
   he touches the mountains, and they smoke.

I will sing to the LORD all my life;
   I will sing praise to my God as long as I live.

May my meditation be pleasing to him,
   as I rejoice in the LORD.

Psalm 104, verses 31–34 (New International Version of the Bible)

The Rt. Revd Jim Thompson, *Bishop of Bath and Wells*

Thou, O heavenly Guide of our devotion and our love,
by teaching us to pray hast shewed us
that Prayer is our Treasury where all blessings are kept,
our Armoury where all our strength and weapons are stored,
the only great preservative,
and the very vital heat of divine love.
Give me grace to call on thee at all times by diligent prayer.
Lord, I know my devotion has daily many unavoidable and
　　unnecessary interruptions,
and I cannot always be actually praying.
All I can do is to beg of thy love to keep my heart always
in an habitual disposition to devotion,
and in mindfulness of thy divine presence.
As thy infinite love is ever-streaming in blessings on me,
O let my soul be ever breathing love to thee. Amen.

From *Exposition of the Catechism* by Thomas Ken,
Bishop of Bath and Wells 1685–91

Here lie I, Martin Elginbrodde:
Hae mercy on my soul, Lord God,
As I would do, were I Lord God
And Ye were Martin Elginbrodde.

An epitaph in Elgin Cathedral

Joanna Trollope, *author*

Lighten our darkness, we beseech thee, O Lord; and by thy great
mercy defend us from all perils and dangers of this night; for the
love of thy only Son, our Saviour, Jesus Christ. Amen.

The Third Collect from Evening Prayer, Book of Common Prayer

Mark Tully, *broadcaster and correspondent from India*

→>–<←

Cast thy bread upon the waters: for thou shalt find it after many
days. Give a portion to seven, and also to eight; for thou
knowest not what evil shall be upon the earth.
If the clouds be full of rain, they empty themselves upon the earth:
and if the tree fall toward the south, or toward the north, in the
place where the tree falleth, there it shall be.
He that observeth the wind shall not sow; and he that regardeth the
clouds shall not reap.
In the morning sow thy seed, and in the evening withhold not thine
hand: for thou knowest not whether shall prosper, either this or
that, or whether they both shall be alike good.

Ecclesiastes 11, verses 1–4 and 6 (Authorized Version)

'I chose these verses, which have remained with me since early schooldays,
because they recall for me both St Ignatius Loyola's prayer "To give and not
to count the cost", and the theme of Krishna's address to Arjun in the *Gita*.'

In liberty from the bonds of attachment, do thou therefore the
work to be done: for the man whose work is pure attains indeed the
Supreme.

Bhagavad Gita, III. 19

The Most Revd Desmond Tutu, *Archbishop Emeritus and Chairperson of the Truth and Reconciliation Commission, South Africa*

→>-<+-

God bless Africa;
Guard her children;
Guide her leaders
And give her peace, for Jesus Christ's sake. Amen.

The Most Revd Trevor Huddleston CR

¶ This prayer is used extensively in the Church of the Province of Southern Africa, and is reproduced here with Archbishop Huddleston's personal acknowledgement.

John Tydeman, *retired Head of Drama, BBC Radio 4*

→>-<+-

Bring us, O Lord God, at our last awakening into the house and gate of heaven; to enter into that gate and dwell in that house, where there shall be no darkness nor dazzling, but one equal light; no noise nor silence, but one equal music; no fears nor hopes, but one equal possession; no ends, nor beginnings, but one equal eternity; in the habitations of thy glory and dominion, world without end. Amen.

John Donne (1572–1631)

Baroness van Randwyck, *musician, linguist, and volunteer castle guide*

→>-<+

Blessings come in many guises
That God alone in love devises,
And sickness which we dread so much
Can bring a very healing touch,
For often on the wings of pain
The peace we sought before in vain
Will come to us with sweet surprise
For God is merciful and wise.
And through long hours of tribulation
God gives us time for meditation,
And no sickness can be counted loss
That teaches us to bear our cross.

Helen Steiner-Rice (1900–81)

I Am Not There

Do not stand at my grave and weep;
I am not there. I do not sleep.
I am a thousand winds that blow;
I am the diamond glints on snow.
I am the sunlight on ripened grain;
I am the gentle autumn rain.
When you awaken in the morning's hush,
I am the swift uplifting rush
Of quiet birds in circled flight.
I am the soft stars that shine at night.
Do not stand at my grave and cry,
I am not there; I did not die.

¶ Left by Stephen Cummins, a soldier killed in an explosion in Northern Ireland, 'to all his loved ones'. This poem is becoming a wide favourite and has been variously attributed to J. T. Wiggins, an English émigré to America, or to one of two Americans, Mary E. Fry and Marianne Reinhart. Others believe it to be a Navajo burial prayer.

Katherine Venning, *organ builder, Durham*

->><-

Generous God, Creator Spirit,
in the making of music
you have given us a delight for the mind and a solace for the heart.
By the harmonies of your grace
resolve the discord of our lives,
that we may sound forth your praise
in all we do and all we are,
to the glory of your great and wonderful name. Amen.

Peter Baelz, Dean Emeritus of Durham Cathedral

Rosemary Verey, *gardener and author*

->><-

O God, who hast prepared for them that love thee such good things as pass man's understanding; Pour into our hearts such love toward thee, that we, loving thee above all things, may obtain thy promises, which exceed all that we can desire; through Jesus Christ our Lord. Amen.

Collect for the sixth Sunday after Trinity, Book of Common Prayer

'When I was at school in 1930–38 we learnt and had to recite each Sunday's collect. A wonderful discipline.'

Major-General Charles Vyvyan, *Head of the British Defence Staff, Washington*

→>-<-

Prayer for a Loved One

Thou who knowest so much and lovest so many, bless, I pray Thee, my dearest love; comfort her and be with her, guide her and be near her; and let Thy light so shine upon her that she may see it and follow it and come at last unto Thy everlasting Kingdom. Amen.

Charles Vyvyan

Command what Thou wilt, but give what Thou commandest; above all things give me the strength to be Thy child on earth as Thou art my Father in Heaven; that in all that I think and say and do I may reflect Thy love, Thy life and Thy understanding. Amen.

Charles Vyvyan

Elizabeth Walrond, *Sunday School teacher, mother and farmer's wife*

→>-<-

Lord Jesus, take me this day and use me.
Take my lips and speak through them.
Take my mind and think through it.
Take my will and act through it,
and fill my heart with love for you.

From *Unto the Hills*

'This is one of our Sunday School Prayers, which we use regularly and which the children each have copies of at home. I love the prayer's commitment of the whole self to God's service.'

John Warburton-Lee, *author, photographer and explorer*

'Poor Don Camillo', whispered the Lord tenderly. And Don Camillo spread out his arms as though he wished to say that he did his best and that if he sometimes made mistakes it was not deliberately.

From *The Little World of Don Camillo* (1951) by Giovanni Guareschi (1908–68)

The Rt. Hon. the Lady Warnock,
House of Lords cross-bencher, philosopher, Chairman of the Committee of Inquiry on Human Fertilisation

Lord Jesus, think on me,
Nor let me go astray;
Through darkness and perplexity
Point Thou the heavenly way.

Lord Jesus, think on me,
When flows the tempest high:
When on doth rush the enemy
O Saviour, be Thou nigh.

Bishop Synesius of Cyrene (Bishop of Ptolemais) (375–430); translated by
Allen W. Chatfield (1808–96)

'I love this, partly for its setting (Southwell from Damon's Psalter, 1579) and partly for its deeply moving interpretation in *Noye's Fludde* by Benjamin Britten. It sends shivers down my spine just to write it out.'

The Rt. Hon. the Lord Weatherill,
former Speaker of the House of Commons

→>-<←

Notice everything.
Correct a little.
Cherish the brethren.

Adapted by Lord Weatherill from the words of St Bernard of Clairvaux (1090–1153), Cistercian mystic and reformer, which were given to him by the Rt. Revd Thomas McMahon, Bishop of Brentwood.

'I used this rule for the 10 years of my speakership. It was quoted by Betty Boothroyd, who said when elected speaker that she would also cherish the Ladies.'

In thought – Faith
In word   – Truth
In deed   – Courage
In life   – Service

'This alternative prayer was given to me by one of my constituents in 1983 and sustained me in good times and bad throughout my speakership.'

❡ These words, whose author cannot be traced, are inscribed on the 146-foot-high Jaipur column which stands in the forecourt of the residence of the President of India (previously the Viceregal Lodge). It commemorates the founding of New Delhi in 1911 and has the added words, 'So may India be great'.

The Westminster Abbey Choristers

✦

O Lord our God, give us by your Holy Spirit a willing heart and a ready hand to use all your gifts to your praise and glory; through Jesus Christ our Lord.

Thomas Cranmer (1489–1556)

I believe in the sun even when it is not shining.
I believe in love even when I cannot feel it.
I believe in God, even when he is silent.

Words found written on the cell wall of a Jewish prisoner in Cologne

O Jesus, Son of God, who was silent before Pilate, do not let us wag our tongues without thinking of what we are to say and how to say it.

Irish Gaelic prayer

¶ These three prayers come from a selection chosen for this anthology by the choristers.

Simon Weston, *former Welsh Guardsman*

Welsh Guards Collect

O Lord God, who has given us the Land of Our Fathers for our inheritance, help Thy servants, The Welsh Guards, to keep Thy laws as our heritage for ever, until we come to that better and heavenly country which Thou hast prepared for us; through Jesus Christ our Lord. Amen.

Matthew Tobias (1880–1962)

❡ Padre Tobias, a loved and outspoken egalitarian, served during the Great War. He wrote many of the Army collects after meticulous research into the regiments' history and traditions.

J. P. R. Williams, *Welsh Rugby Union international player 1969–1981, consultant orthopaedic surgeon*

Love divine, all loves excelling,
Joy of Heaven, to earth come down,
Fix in us Thy humble dwelling,
All Thy faithful mercies crown;
Jesu, Thou art all compassion,
Pure unbounded love Thou art;
Visit us with Thy salvation,
Enter every trembling heart.

Charles Wesley (1707–88)

'This hymn by Charles Wesley was sung in six-part harmony to the tune Blaenwern at my father's funeral.'

Michael Williams, *actor*

→>·<←

O, Sacred Heart of Jesus,
I place my trust in Thee.

'This traditional prayer was contained in a booklet given to students at my school, St Edward's College, Liverpool, by the teaching order, the Christian Brothers.'

The Revd Trevor Williams, *Leader of the Corrymeela Community, an ecumenical community of reconciliation in Northern Ireland*

→>·<←

Give us, Lord God, a vision of our world as your love would make
   it:
a world where the weak are protected, and none go hungry or poor;
a world where the benefits of civilized life are shared, and everyone
   can enjoy them;
a world where different races, nations and cultures live in tolerance
   and mutual respect;
a world where peace is built with justice, and justice is guided by
   love;
And give us the inspiration and courage to build it, through Jesus
   Christ our Lord. Amen.

Trevor Williams

'There are no quick fixes in the work of Reconciliation, it is a web of "right relationships". One break destroys the whole. To work for peace you need a clear vision to maintain your energy and nourish your hope. The love of God alone brings this about.'

Sir John Wills, *Lord Lieutenant of Somerset*

→>-<←

O God, who knowest us to be set in the midst of so many and great dangers, that by reason of the frailty of our nature we cannot always stand upright; Grant to us such strength and protection, as may support us in all dangers, and carry us through all temptations; through Jesus Christ our Lord. Amen.

Collect for the fourth Sunday after Epiphany, Book of Common Prayer

'This prayer speaks to those who seek strength to meet personal challenges with a steadfast heart.'

Stanley Wooderson, *Olympic runner, mile and half-mile world record holder, 1937*

→>-<←

O God, from whom all holy desires, all good counsels, and all just works do proceed; Give unto thy servants that peace which the world cannot give; that both our hearts may be set to obey thy commandments, and also that by thee we being defended from the fear of our enemies may pass our time in rest and quietness; through the merits of Jesus Christ our Saviour. Amen.

The Second Collect at Evening Prayer, Book of Common Prayer

Harold Wright, *retired thatcher*

✦➤◄✦

Rock of ages, cleft for me,
Let me hide myself in thee;
Let the water and the blood,
From thy riven side which flowed,
Be of sin the double cure:
Cleanse me from its guilt and power.

Augustus M. Toplady (1740–78)

¶ Mr Wright is the fourth-generation thatcher since James Wright, 1781–1865. A son
and a grandson are also thatching in Compton Dundon, Somerset.

The Rt. Revd Abbot Timothy Wright,
Abbot of Ampleforth

When God Made You

When
God
made
you
there
was
silence
in
heaven
for
five
minutes.
Then
God
said:
'How come I never thought of that before?'

From *Perhaps God* (1985) by Ralph Wright OSB

'This prayer by my brother attracts me because it highlights the truth that only God can understand the uniqueness which is each one of us.'

Paul Young,
Chief Fire Officer, Somerset Fire Brigade

+>-<+

Whenever we are called to serve you, Lord,
wherever fires rage, or folk are trapped,
give us strength to save a life, whoever it may be.
Help us to rescue a little child before it is too late,
or to save an older person too frail to escape.
Enable us to be alert and hear the weakest cry
or quickly and efficiently put fires out.
We want to fill our calling, Lord,
to serve our neighbours in their need.
If one of us should fall and lose our life,
then bless with your all-embracing love
those who are dearest to us.
We ask all this trusting in Jesus Christ. Amen.

¶ This is based on 'The Firefighter's Prayer', which is said at funerals, major parades and services. It was recently read at the memorial service for Nigel Musselwhite, OBE, who was known throughout the Fire Service for his good humour and leadership.

Postscript

Prayer is like a mountain. On its lower slopes are many wonderful individual prayers which express the needs of a particular moment or circumstance in life. But as we climb towards the summit, I believe we come to just two thoughts, which distil the very essence of what all prayer is about. Each can make up a very short prayer in itself, to be inwardly repeated again and again, like the 'Jesus prayer'.

The first is 'God have mercy on me'. This expresses our sense of separation from God: the way we are isolated in our ego-self, which is what the idea of sin is all about, how in ourselves we are endlessly imperfect and unworthy. Through this repeated thought we try to dissolve the separation between that hard, finite little pebble of our own limited consciousness and the infinite power of love and perfection which is both beyond us and deep within us, because it is everywhere and eternal.

Through this first prayer we may come to the second. This is simply the all-embracing thought, 'God, I love you', almost like breathing – although here we are passing beyond words. On the rare occasions when we can reach that state, we sense 'One-ness' – that complete living unity of all things, visible and invisible, of which Dante wrote when he ended his *Divine Comedy* on a vision of 'the love that moves the sun and the other stars'.

When we emerge from such a state, and come back down the mountain, to face again 'all the chances and changes of this fleeting world', we can never entirely lose an inner certainty that, in the end, whatever happens, 'all shall be well and all manner of thing shall be well'.

Christopher Booker, author and journalist

The Threshold Prize

Registered Charity: 1058886

Now, more than ever, with the strictures of the new curriculum and the stresses of modern society, children need the stimulus and solace of creative writing. The Threshold Prize does not simply encourage children who have an urge to write, but reaches out to those who might otherwise never realize a talent for, and love of, writing. In order to achieve this, writers who are skilled not only in writing themselves but also in communicating with children run workshops in schools, and other writers act as adjudicators (Margaret Drabble for 1997 and Victoria Glendinning for 1998). It is tremendously rewarding for children and their teachers to know that their work has been judged by highly regarded authors.

The Threshold Prize, conceived in 1995, is now in its second operational year in Somerset and North Somerset. Run by a group of trustees, with the help of the local education authorities, it involves over 1000 children from a mixture of urban and rural areas. It is hoped that the concept of the prize will spread to other areas.

The royalties from this book will be donated to the Threshold Prize, which is voluntarily financed. Donations can also be sent to: Ian Boage and Co., Chartered Accountants, Little Hamdown, Picts Hill, Langport, Somerset, TA10 9EX, or to Lady Cassidi, Threshold Prize, c/o Battens Solicitors, Church Street, Yeovil, Somerset, BA20 1HB.

FAVOURITE PRAYERS

Subject Index

Index of Contributors

Index of First Lines

Index of Authors and Sources

Acknowledgements

Every effort has been made to locate copyright holders, although in a small number of cases this has proved impossible. We are grateful for permission to reprint the following copyright material. We also thank individuals who sent their own prayers.

Extracts from the Authorized Version of the Bible (The King James Bible), the rights in which are vested in the Crown, are reproduced by permission of the Crown's Patentee, Cambridge University Press.

Extracts from The Book of Common Prayer, the rights in which are vested in the Crown, are reproduced by permission of the Crown's Patentee, Cambridge University Press.

Scripture quotations from the New King James Version are reproduced by permission of Thomas Nelson, © 1979, 1980, 1982.

Scripture quotations from the Holy Bible New International Version, © 1973, 1978, 1984 by International Bible Society, are reproduced by permission of Hodder & Stoughton.

Scripture quotations from the Jerusalem Bible © 1966, 1967, 1968 are reproduced by permission of Darton Longman and Todd, and Doubleday.

Prayer from The Prayer Book as Proposed in 1928 by permission of The Central Board of Finance of the Church of England.

Scripture quotations from the Amplified Bible are reproduced by permission of the Lockman Foundation.

Prayers from the Authorised Daily Prayer Book are reproduced by permission of the Singer's Prayer Book Publication Committee of the United Synagogue.

Prayer from the Alternative Service Book 1980 is copyright © The Central Board of Finance of the Church of England and is reproduced with permission.

Prayers from The Bhagavad Gita, translated by Juan Mascaro (Penguin Classics, 1962), © Juan Mascaro, are reproduced by permission of Penguin UK.

Extracts from Essence of Good Fortune are reproduced by permission of the Manjushri Mahayana Buddhist Centre and the Madhyamak Buddhist Centre

Prayers from the Worship Book of the World Council of Churches, reproduced by permission of the Anglican Church in Aotearoa, New Zealand and Polynesia

The following items are arranged in order of appearance in the book:

R. L. Sharpe: Doubleday, for 'A Bag of Tools', from *Best-Loved Poems of the American People*, edited by Hazel Feldman (1936)

Kahlil Gibran: The National Committee of Gibran, for words from *The Prophet* (1951)

Ogden Nash: André Deutsch for 'Beneath This Slab'

Frank Borman: A Prayer Offered in Space, by permission of the author

Phyllis Krystal: 'Please think through me', by permission of the author

Lionel Blue: 'The Just Society' from *Forms of Prayer for Jewish Worship*, vol.1, *Daily, Sabbath and Occasional Prayers*, by permission of the Reform Synagogues of Great Britain

Ronald Blythe : 'A Suffolk Prayer'

Helen Waddell (trans.): Constable, for prayer by Sedulius Scottus

Andre Zirnheld: Little, Brown, for 'I Bring This Prayer to You, Lord', from *David Stirling: A Biography*, by Alan Hoe; also Professor Alan Steele for the translation, and the L'Amicale des Anciens Parachutistes SAS et des Anciens Commandos de la France libre

Roy Calne: Calder, for 'The Creator's Testament to Modern Man', from *Sir Roy Calne: Too Many People*

Dag Hammarskjold: Faber and Faber, for three prayers from *Markings*, translated by W. H. Auden

Charles Tett: Christian Industrial Training Centres (Nairobi, Kenya), for 'The Master Carpenter'; also Toc H and the Iona Community for prayers of similar wording

Eugene Greco: Kingsway's Thankyou Music, for 'Teach Me Your Ways, O Lord My God' © 1990

Herbert E. Palmer: J. M. Dent, for 'Prayer for Rain', from *The Vampire*

Dietrich Bonhoeffer: SCM Press Ltd, for 'O God, early in the morning', from *Morning Prayers* (1971)

T. S. Eliot: Faber and Faber, for lines of Choruses from 'The Rock X', from *Collected Poems 1909-1962*

Carolyn Martin (compiler): Hodder and Stoughton, for two graces from *A Book of Graces* (1980)

Dick Francis: Michael Joseph, for a prayer first published in *Straight* (1989)William Barclay: HarperCollins, for 'In the Morning', from *A Plain Man's Book of Prayer*

Martin Luther King: Intellectual Properties Management Inc., for 'Everybody can be great', from *Words of Martin Luther King*

David Caccia: his family for 'I don't want to be the Christ, dear Lord'

Elizabeth Basset: Darton Longman and Todd, for an extract from *Love Is My Meaning* © 1973, 1986

The Scots Guards for their Regimental Collect

Michel Quoist: Gill & Macmillan, for 'Green Blackboards', from *Prayers of Life*

David Goldstein(trans.): David Higham Associates, for 'Let Man Remember', from *The Jewish Poets of Spain*

David Adam: SPCK, for 'Come Holy Dove', from *Border Lands*

Ronald Knox: Search Press, for 'O sacred head ill-used'

Alexander Carmichael: Scottish Academic Press, for 'Coistrig Mathar', from *Carmina Gadelica, Volumes 1 and 2*

William Gaither: Kingsway's Thankyou Music for 'Because He Lives' © 1971

John Gillespie Magee: *This England* (quarterly), for 'High Flight'

A. E. Housman: The Society of Authors, for 'Easter Hymn'

Charles Boyd: A.R. Mowbray, for 'Have mercy, O most gracious God, 'from *Help to Worship*

Dylan Thomas: David Higham Associates, for an extract from *A Child's Christmas in Wales*, published by J. M. Dent

Mrs J. R. Youens, for 'A Prayer for the Gurkha'

Mary Louise Haskins: Sheil Land Associates, for 'The Gate of the Year'

Dorothy M. Stewart (complier): Lion Press, for 'The Gift of Silence', from *Women of Prayer*

Michael Sadgrove: 'Death of a Child' a 'A Coventry Prayer'

Stephen Pope: 'The Hermit'

John Galsworthy: Halsey Meyer Higgins, for 'If on a Spring Night'

Craig Adams: HM Prison Service, for 'Help Me to Take the Right Path'

SCM Press, for 'Bless us, O God, with the vision of Thy Being'. from *A Devotional Diary* by J.H. Oldham (1925)

Rudyard Kipling: A. P. Watt on behalf of The National Trust, for lines from 'If'

Rosemary Turnbull: 'The Glastonbury Prayer'

J. B. Goodliffe: SCM Press, for a prayer from *School Prayers* © 1927

Thomas Merton: Search Press and Burns & Oates, for 'My Lord God, I have no idea where I am going'

Tukaram: Prinit Press, for 'Of what avail this restless hurrying' from *Tukaram: Indian Peasant and Mystic*, edited by J. Hyland

Idries Shah: Octagon Press, for 'A Sufi Prayer', reprinted from *The Way of Sufi*

George MacLed: The Iona Community, for 'O Christ, you are within each of us'

Joyce Grenfell: Macmillan, for 'If I Should Go Before the Rest of You'

David Stancliffe: The Central Board of Finance of the Church of England, for 'Blessed Are You, Lord Our God', from *The Promise of His Glory* © 1990, 1991

Covenant Prayer: Methodist Publishing House

G. Betty Hares: 'O Christ the Light' by permission of the author

'Desdemona's Prayer Before Her Death': Calder Publications, ENO Guide no. 7

Trevor Huddleston: 'God Bless Africa' by permission of the author

Helen Steiner-Rice: Random House, for 'Blessings Come in Many Guises', from *Daily Reflections*

Peter Baelz: 'Generous God, Creator Spirit'. by permission of the author

R. R. Broackes (compiler): SPCK, for 'Take Me This Day and Use Me', from *Unto the Hills* (1958)

Giles Harcourt (compiler): HarperCollins, for 'I Believe in the Sun', from *Short Prayers for the Long Day*

Matthew Tobias: The Welsh Guards, for their regimental colect